BARE BREASTS

BARE BREASTS
The Untold Story of a Zambian Journalist

DAVID KASHIKI

BARE BREASTS
© 2017 by David Kashiki

All rights reserved. No part of this book may be reproduced in any form without written permission from the publisher, except in the case of brief quotations embodied in critical articles or reviews.

ISBN: 9781973200048

Book and Cover design by George Lonswana

To order additional copies of this book,
or for comments contact:
+260 954 587 364
barebreasts1@gmail.com

*This book has been
dedicated with love to
my mother, my siblings
and Journalists striving
to truthfully and impartially
inform society*

Contents

Acknowledgements	ix
PREFACE	xi
FOREWORD	xiii

CHAPTER ONE — 1

The Post Genesis	1
Face-to-face with Fred M'membe	6
A step into the Post got me beaten	10
Flying with the Scotts	18
No picture was worth my life	22
My 'bloody 2016 Youth Day present'	28
The bullet that sent Post Journalists running	32
Police at 'war' with UPND cadres	34
Apprehended and detained at Kabwata Police Station	38
For how long will M'membe 'insult' the President?	40

CHAPTER TWO — 45

Journey from church to Dundumwezi	45
QUIT! A test of comradeship	47

CHAPTER THREE — 51

Bare breasts in front of my camera	51
Dancing with the President: music and politics in Zambia	55

CHAPTER FOUR — 63

Reportage and objectivity in Zambian media — 63
M'membe *ayamba* Chagwa, Post *Yagwa* (The Inside View) — 68
Police brutality — 92
An ex-con and the closure of *The Post* — 96
M'membe, Kabimba and the formation of the Rainbow Party — 100

CHAPTER FIVE — 109

Poor wages: A cause of compromised and unprofessional media — 109
Zambia in dire need of youth leadership — 113

CHAPTER SIX — 117

Cameraman turns Joy FM & Prime TV proprietor — 117
The audience will determine the future of news — 121

CHAPTER SEVEN — 125

The election of an accomplished liar — 125
Unemployment, *'Wako ni Wako'* in governments — 130
The end of a lying politician — 133

AUTOBIOGRAPHY — 137

REFERENCES — 139

ACKNOWLEDGEMENTS

THIS work would not have been feasible without the help of several people. I feel indebted to my family; my phenomenal mother, brothers and sisters, for showing unwavering support during my day-to-day practice of journalism. I am grateful to my friends who made precious suggestions to my script.

To my manuscript editors Wana Kalala and Chambwa Moonga, book cover designer/editor and typesetter George Lonswana, and Jonas Zimba for the legal guidance, to you all—I am most grateful.

Photo credits: The cover picture of the author in a tussle with suspected PF cadres was taken by a brave photojournalist and my colleague Tobias Phiri. His vigilance on duty earned him this historic picture. I thank you most sincerely.

The author made all efforts to ascertain the identity of the photographer of the cover picture of Fred M'membe, but this could not be done by the time of publication. Still, I humbly thank the unknown photographer.

For the many pictures used in this book, special credit goes to Melony Chisanga and Salim Dawood photojournalists who are a rising talent in the world of photography.

PREFACE

I WRITE this book as a young Zambian author and in my capacity as a former Post journalist who believes that the greatness of my country lies in patriotism, integrity in leadership, the promotion of freedom of expression, the right to information, and the support of entrepreneurship.

This book, bare breasts the truth (lays truth bare) and untold stories relating to journalism and politics in Zambia. It has been inspired by the day-to-day experiences of Zambian journalists and was birthed with a vision to help society comprehend the various trends characterising the profession and politics.

You as a reader in particular, shall be able to deduce and appreciate Zambian journalism and the political arena in which it operates.

To any would-be journalists, you will never learn in your entire journalism or mass communications course what you will find in this book.

This book provides you with numerous practical accounts of the Zambian 'outside-class' journalism. For the reader who is simply curious to know more about issues surrounding this country's socio-political and journalistic arena in the 21st century, I guarantee that your curiosity will be satisfied as I will take you through a thrilling journalism, political and entrepreneurial setup of this country.

In short, this book uncovers and lays bare issues you may not have realised existed.

However, note that, issues discussed in this book are not meant to injure anyone as I am alive to the fact that, we are all human prone to err, we are mortal beings. This piece of literature acts as lessons to would-be media entity owners or general business proprietors.

It also acts as a medium for a journalist like me, to communicate to leaders in my country; challenges or misunderstandings a journalist is faced with in the course of disbursing duties to the nation. Also, the book's intention is to help stir change in the way journalism is being practiced; subjectively.

Opinions and observations made in this book are entirely my own, and do not in any way represent those of the institution I may currently be working for, or a group of associates/friends.

FOREWORD

It has been a privilege for me to read the manuscript form of this book written by a young journalist David Kashiki, who spent some years working for the independent Post Newspaper, before it was forced out of business. He has gone through a lot of varied experiences in his short professional life. Some of the accounts he has given in this book are hair raising, horrifying, hilarious, sad and even controversial.

As an author myself, I know how difficult it is to write a book of this nature and about events or people who are still alive and who have their own recollections of the same events, which may differ from yours. This is normal and to be expected.

I have always encouraged my countrymen and women with rich and educative experiences to write books and share their experiences for the benefit of generations yet unborn and for posterity. It is disappointing that very few of us have committed pen to paper. I am painfully aware that no matter how a book of this nature is written, there are bound to be people who will be unhappy, angry and even disagree with certain aspects of its contents. I admire the courage of the author and the amount of effort he has put into it.

Trying to draw the right balance in books of this nature is not easy, let alone achieve consensus. This remains every author's nightmare all over the world. The awareness of this elephant in the room, is however not sufficient to prevent the writing and publishing of books of this nature. It raises many issues including the enormous risks journalists take to cover certain events, particularly those of a political nature.

The book also raises fundamental issues of whether society really understands the role of journalists and the need to give them adequate space to do their work professionally. I hold no brief from the author as to the accuracy of its contents or interpretation. That lies with the author.

All I can say, is that, it is an interesting book worth reading, which brings out certain vital information I did not know or had forgotten. It also underlines the inherent dangers journalists face in the discharge of their duties to inform, educate and entertain their readers. I hope the book will also inspire and encourage other journalists to write and share their experiences.

Dr Vernon J. Mwaanga
Lusaka, October, 2017

CHAPTER ONE

The Post Genesis

WITH editorial ideas borrowed from the then South Africa's liberal newspaper, T*he Weekly Mail,* and a Lisbon new daily publication dubbed, *Publico*, 32-year-old Fred M'membe and 29-year-old Malawian born journalist, Mike Hall, among others, managed to put the first-ever 30, 000 copies of the Weekly Post on the streets of Lusaka and the Copperbelt. The paper sold out within three hours of being on the streets owing to 'juicy' stories it carried. Helped by the first-ever crop of reporters, Jowie Mwiinga, the late Chris Chitanda, and Dingi Chirwa; Pascalina Phiri, Mann Banda, and Wam Kwalayela as sub-edtitors, and Robby Makayi as the paper's first editor, *The Weekly Post* gained its respect.

It started as a weekly newspaper on July 26, 1991 and was published by Post Newspapers Limited under the name, "*The Weekly Post*". *The Weekly Post*, which was circulated on Fridays, was co-founded by Mike Hall, Fred M'membe, Masautso Phiri, and John Mukela. The newspaper subsequently became a daily tabloid on October 23, 1995.

Having noticed the United Independence Party (UNIP) regime's massive control of national newspapers, Mike Hall, now bureau chief for *Bloomberg News* in South and Southeast Asia, and Masautso Phiri, then a researcher at the United States Embassy in Lusaka, birthed the initial idea of *The Post* in the early 1990s while having lunch at the Great Wall of China in Lusaka.

Registered on February 28, 1991, the company delimited shareholding to not more than 15 per cent per individual shareholder, a restriction that aimed at restraining those that may have had more shares against holding the paper at ransom when faced with editorial differences.

It is cardinal to note here that the formation of *The Post* took four of its co-founders almost a year of planning its birth, and only took a few days for Andrew Herbert Chiwenda, Roy Habaalu, Bonaventure Bwalya, Mwendalubi Mweene and Abel Mboozi to file a petition that resulted in the company being placed under liquidation. The former Post workers' reason for filing a petition was that, the company had failed to pay them their benefits. The company argued that, it was ready to pay the said workers, but, the action was not reversed.

The Post was started with an initial capital of $25,000, and when it was launched, it happened to be one of the primary newspapers in the country during the last days of Kenneth David Kaunda's UNIP regime.

Post Co-founder, Mike Hall, in his write up to commemorate years of The *Post*'s existence in 2004, stated that, when he and Phiri realised that if the paper they were planning to establish was to be financially viable, they needed someone with expertise in financial management, and at this point they wondered whom it could be.

"...*Weeks earlier, I remembered meeting an unusual accountant in unusual circumstances. I had been tear-gassed during a riot in Choma covering the trial of Frederick Chiluba. This accountant [Fred M'membe] took pity on me and Melinda Ham, then the only foreign correspondents in Zambia, and gave us a lift to Lusaka. I remembered trying to sleep, listening to the driver talk about his boredom with the accounting profession - he was an auditor at KPMG - his interest in politics, excitement at the pro-democracy movement, student days in London and his commitment to Zambia. He made a big impression on me. Weeks later, though, I couldn't remember his name until one day outside the High Court. My second meeting with Fred M'membe was the beginning of a long journey and deep friendship.*

"*I told him of our plan and asked for his help, offering to pay for it. Fred was blunt: 'You can't afford to pay me', he said "But I'll give you free advice to get you started. Fred's advice very quickly turned to full-scale involvement and he became the fourth co-founder of the project. We were committed to one basic principle from the start: the paper had to be independent. We didn't want any one owner or group of owners dictating what we printed,"* reads part of Hall's write up published in The Post newspaper in 2004.

"*We designed a prospectus to attract a diverse group of investors. Fred had no experience of newspapers and I had no experience of finance. For weeks we sat together, often late into the early hours, planning details, examining costs and doing cash-flow and profit and loss projections. Fred taught me some basics. 'Do you know a business can make a profit, but still go bankrupt?' I remember him asking. I said that didn't make sense. 'Cash-flow', he said, "You've got to have enough cash at any one time to keep the business running.' Fred became more involved than any of us in the project. He took unpaid leave from his well-paying job and eventually resigned to work full-time as Managing Director of Post Newspapers Ltd., which was then nothing more than a piece of paper and a vision. Masautso carried on working as a researcher and joined the paper as a full-time writer with the title of Special Projects Editor in 1993. I continued reporting for the BBC, while John, who was to have been the paper's first editor, decided to pursue an offer of further education in Britain. He returned about a year later to edit the paper briefly before leaving again. We started meeting prominent, progressive people who we thought might buy shares in the company. It was a hard sell and* it was important we were seen to be professional: we held meetings of prospective shareholders, wrote reports and letters and answered scores of questions about the paper's viability.

"Fred's experience as an auditor was critical to persuading our potential shareholders that we could make the paper financially viable. Without his connections, powers of persuasion and determination, the project wouldn't have got off the ground..." Hall remarked.

Among the people credited with making it possible for the Post Newspapers Limited to take off were freedom fighter Simon Zukas, former vice-president, Enoch Kavindele, then a UNIP central committee member, Theo Bull, late Baldwin Nkumbula, late United Party for National Development (UPND) founding president; at this time, head of the Anglo American Corporation, Anderson Kambele Mazoka, late Movement For Multi-Party Democracy founder member Arthur Wina and prominent lawyer Sakwiba Sikota, who is credited with helping with formalities of registering the company.

It is clear that, M'membe's commitment and enormous involvement in the management of *The Post* business eventually earned him shares, which he acquired from major shareholders. The acquisition of major shares subsequently made him a major shareholder, and editor-in-chief of the newspaper with about 49,589.00 ordinary shares, as of November 4, 2016.

It is an undeniable fact that *The Post* under M'membe gave those that wielded power sleepless nights with its investigative and brave stance on societal issues and exposition of corruption. The newspaper was arguably the people's favourite as it gave them, mostly those that were fade up of first president, Kaunda's 27 year reign, a platform to air their grievances and access information of relief.

Through tough and tested photojournalists in the likes of Sheikh Chifuwe, Thomas Nsama, Eddie Mwanaleza, Collins Phiri, Salim Dawood, Manfred Musanshi, Joseph Mwenda, Angela Ntentabunga, among other, *The Post* proved that seeing, was actually believing. Through their impactful and controversial pictures in *The Post*, photojournalism in

CHAPTER ONE

Zambia was greatly shaped into what it is today. Their pictures indeed told a story worth a thousand words.

Post Newspapers Limited was closed on June 21, 2016, through an action ostensibly by the Zambia Revenue Authority under the guide of pursuing payment of tax arrears and subsequently liquidated on November 3, 2016. However, long before the company was placed under liquidation, the Tax Appeals Tribunal ordered the tax collectors to hand Post properties until a full appeal was heard. The order was disregarded and the newspaper's property remained under seizure until the Lusaka High Court placed it under receivership, and appointed lawyer, Lewis Chisanga Mosho of Messrs Lewis Nathan Advocate, as provisional liquidator.

"It is hereby ordered that Lewis Mosho of Messrs Lewis Nathan Advocate, be and is, hereby appointed to act as Provisional Liquidator in respect of all the assets and properties of the Respondent in the winding up proceedings herein..." read part of an exparte order issued by the High Court.

In its over 25 years of existence, *The Post* once bragged of having had a circulation of about 60,000, making it arguably, the first privately owned newspaper with a wide reach in different corners of the country. During the heydays of *The Post*, whenever a rumour of public interest went viral in the country, the newspaper was what people awaited to confirm if what they may have heard was true. It became a tabloid to cross-check the truth that people may have heard taking turns on the streets, public transport, and possibly, in the airspace. The newspaper's name gained more popularity when it published President Edgar Lungu's speech to the 5th session of the 11th National Assembly, before he delivered it. This was not the first time that the newspaper published documents like the National Budget, way before being presented to parliament. For this quality, the newspaper was the people's choice. The paper was arguably considered to have played a major role in changing the politics of Zambia, a Southern African country once subjected to a one party system of governance.

The Post may be said to have died, but, the question that lingers on most of its followers' minds is: has "the paper that digs deeper" really died? If it has died, will it reincarnate or perhaps, it lives amongst us? Some chitchat and say, "The ghost of *The Post* is amongst us and it will not rest until it consumes the killers of the newspaper".

But, the million dollar question is: is this the ultimate end of *The Post*? Who knows? *The Post* may come back sooner or later. And its missions would be clear, and among them, to deal with those it perceived to have forcibly put it into hibernation.

Face-to-face with Fred M'membe

"Why are you a vegan?" I once asked him. His response, simple yet profound, left me mesmerised. "It is healthy and it makes you strong," he said. "Look at the biggest and most powerful animal on land - the elephant. It's vegetarian and it is very strong. When you eat beef - red meat - it takes between 24-72 hours to be digested and therefore, the prolonged digestion process drains much of your energy, and that is the energy which is supposed to be directed at thinking and working, not sleeping. So instead of eating beef and waiting for it to digest, I'm vegan. Look at the lion: when it eats, it sleeps an average of 20 hours a day, and its strength to prey on other animals lies in its pride."

I had asked this when several Post journalists and I were having lunch at the staff canteen. M'membe had joined us at the table and after we had exchanged pleasantries, he asked about what was in the news on that particular day. We shared the day's news items with him and he gave us his opinion on the choice of news stories. It was then I realised the uniqueness in the way M'membe led his life. He didn't drink alcohol and was vegetarian. I had been itching to find out where he drew the inspiration to lead such a 'smart' life. And so I asked him that question, and his response both humbled and inspired me.

I was able to learn more about his unique character. He once drank alcohol, but quit. His life while at *The Post*, revolved around constantly studying and reading. He prided knowledge, his office full of writing by different authors. In his over 25 years of journalism practice, M'membe worked 24/7. And throughout his time at *The Post* as an editor-in-chief, he reported for work early in the morning and knocked off very late, often after witnessing the designing and laying out of the following day's edition.

I first came across Fred M'membe in February 2014, when I was being interviewed for the position of photojournalist. And I must share that, the first encounter was quite memorable. I was literally left amazed by his actions towards myself and the other unsuccessful interviewees.

The first time I set foot on The Post Newspapers premises on the famous Bwinjimfumu Road was when I took a letter applying for a placement in the company following an advert in the paper for a photojournalist.

My second visit came when I was called, along with five other candidates, to be interviewed for the position.

So as the six of us awaited to enter the interview room, M'membe, wearing a green cadet cap, a chequered light-blue long sleeved shirt, blue jeans, and converse, walked into the small newsroom where we had been asked to wait for Beston Hangoma, The Post human resources officer.

Beston was tasked to screen our documents and lead us to a panel of interviewers, that comprised former Post senior general manager, Sheik Chifuwe, former Deputy Managing Editor Speedwell Mupuchi, and Yobe Nkuwa, among other senior officers.

With utmost courtesy, M'membe greeted each one of the 'visitors'. As he reached out to shake my hand, I stood up. "How are you, sir?" I said, a tad nervous.

"Don't call me sir," he said with a gentle wry smile. "I've not been knighted by the Queen. I'm Fred."

His response vividly resounded in my head.

Prior to him introducing himself as M'membe, I had wondered who the man in the green cap was. I didn't know he was the renowned Fred

M'membe. In my mind, M'membe was this huge, dark person, with a gloomy expression. Instead, his stature and complexion was the exact opposite of what I had often envisioned him to be. My sense of imagination had totally betrayed me.

Many people that had not met M'membe pictured him differently. Some thought he was a bi-spectacled person who was always in dapper suits. Others, like me, imagined a fierce task master, whom employees scampered away from whenever they saw him. But all this was far from the truth. My face-to-face encounter and subsequent interactions with M'membe proved my previous imaginations and thoughts wrong. M'membe is an approachable down-to-earth journalist, lawyer and accountant. However, he can be tough and is a strong believer of his own views; it's not easy to change an opinion held by M'membe.

During my time at the Post, I came to know and understand the man better. Aside being very serious with what he had been doing for over 25 years, Fred M'membe is a very jovial person; an excellent and critical thinker so much so that most people that had not met him before found difficult to comprehend when they finally encountered him. Blessed with the ability to relate with the most ordinary person in society, as well as the most powerful, M'membe easily mingled with workers.

This fact reminds me of a story I found at the Post, and was shared with me by my former workmate and colleague, Salim Dawood. This story is of a worker at the company that was summoned to the institution's headquarters to be questioned over some alleged misconduct. The employee was based on the Copperbelt and had never met M'membe since joining the institution. On the day of his arrival, he was drunk and reeking of alcohol. Having arrived at lunch time, he proceeded to the canteen where he happened to sit directly opposite M'membe.

M'membe's dress code quite often disguised his identity. He mostly wore jeans and checked shirts, making him look like an ordinary employee at the institution. So as the unsuspecting employee enjoyed his meal, he asked M'membe, who Fred was, and how he had heard that the editor-in-chief was a difficult person. When he asked this, M'membe

CHAPTER ONE

just smiled. The gentleman asked M'membe, "Do I smell of alcohol?"

Other employees in the canteen simply watched in trepidation as the drama unfolded. The inebriated employee said he had travelled all the way to Lusaka to "sort out" M'membe. But M'membe remained calm and just watched the man. After finishing his meal, M'membe excused himself and left the table. The other employees walked over to their drunk colleague and informed him that he had in fact been talking to Fred M'membe himself. I would have loved to have seen the expression on his face when he was told this. I'm told though that the employee stopped eating, got up and left the canteen. He was never heard from again.

However, efforts to trace the authenticity of this story, proved somewhat difficult, as others said, the story was fictitious.

Anyhow, one major characteristic I respect Fred M'membe for is his genuine belief in the power women have to contribute to the growth of a country's political and socio-economic set-up. At his former company, M'membe struck a balance in promoting workers—both male and female—to managerial positions in almost all departments. He is an advocate of women participation in the management of company affairs. And at national level, his advocacy for women's involvement in matters of governance was undeniable.

At the Post, M'membe had respect for the woman folk, and treated them with utmost courtesy. When he found you telling a story to a group of fellow employees, he would sneak in a joke and say, "*Alemibepa inshi uyu mambala* [what lies is this crook telling you]?" Then he would proceed to greet all the female workers first, followed by the men. This he did literally every day irrespective of his mood.

And whenever Post employees performed exceptionally well, he would personally congratulate them on doing a good job. M'membe took great pride in the company's photojournalists, because he believed, "Are the most intelligent journalists that house skills to get a story in most complicated situations owing to their alertness to every detail during an assignment". During one diary meeting, I recall him saying,

"Photojournalists are the most intelligent journalists that have skills to get a story in most complicated situations owing to their alertness to every detail during an assignment"..

His comment came in the wake of a picture that had impressed him and had a caption that told a better story than the one written by the reporter assigned to do so.

My view on M'membe's character is that he loves what he does. He loves journalism and he will never give up on it. I acknowledge that he may have 'mismanaged' the company in some areas and made poor decisions, but believe me, those that may have forcibly caused the closure of *The Post* and rejoiced in it, may be dealt with in future. Fred M'membe, some of you may not be aware, helped so many people-who were on the Post payroll, until they found their feet. This includes those in government today. He not only supported or advertised some aspiring parliamentary candidates in his newspaper; M'membe did also help many of them with finances.

And today, most of these people rejoice seeing him tormented by some forces. But, like M'membe often told us after the closure of *The Post*, success is achieved in the furnace of humiliation.

A step into the Post got me beaten

Reeking of sweat and alcohol, they surrounded me and roughed me up. Visions of ugly and dark knuckles slamming into my face reverberated in my head. I literally saw stars with each punch that landed on target.

Reflections of how a horde of agitated youths, dressed in all green and pulling and tearing my T-shirt, flooded my terrified mind.

Riot police techniques of combating 'crime', facing and enduring coarse and often foul language were frequent episodes I encountered in the field of Zambia's media industry.

This was the brutality I experienced while on duty. At some point, I mused at how this was not what I had been taught in journalism school.

CHAPTER ONE

"My lecturer probably never mentioned that there would be such events for a reason," I said to myself. "I never heard of anyone complain about harsh political and police harassment until I experienced it."

I eventually reasoned that my tutors, probably fearful I would abandon my course, decided against telling me that the profession I had chosen would sometimes lead me into environments that were as hostile as a war zone.

But I continued reflecting on the continued harassment of journalists by police officers and political party cadres. Every time my work colleagues recounted—often comically—my encounters in the pursuit of documenting events and gathering stories, I would experience a quick rise in my blood pressure.

This topic naturally exhumed memories in the sub-conscious. The memories were always frightening. They reminded me of how those youths tore my clothes and took turns assaulting me.

Nonetheless, my heart was unsettled until I decided to break the silence and share the story of my life and experience as a photojournalist.

Photojournalism in Zambia and many other parts of the world is not only demanding but also quite challenging and thrilling. One needs to be at the scene of events as they are unfolding to either get a story or photograph a moment for posterity.

It's worth mentioning that in this profession, some journalists can get a scoop by phone from the comfort of their air-conditioned offices. But a photojournalist, like me, is employed to get into the mix of things and capture that decisive—possibly historic—moment.

Photojournalists are most likely to face dangerous situations, as theirs, inevitably involves fieldwork.

Photojournalism is a challenging and thrilling job in my country.

Taking newsworthy pictures of people and events is not as easy as a journalism student may be taught. First, one needs to be able to exercise news judgment. One also needs to have courage, say, to take a picture of police officers raiding a drug den, people fighting in the community or a notable public figure with one of his concubines in a slum. One needs to have courage and alertness of mind when taking pictures at an accident scene and also be able to help the injured in the event that paramedics don't arrive on site on time.

So this is how it all began.

In secondary school, I had hoped to study law but due to insufficient finances, I could not make it to law school and instead enrolled for a journalism course.

I was accepted to pursue a Diploma in journalism at the Zambia Institute of Mass Communication Educational Trust (ZAMCOM) where I studied from 2011 to 2013.

While in college, I was attached to the *Zambia Daily Mail* newspaper for a number of months on industrial practice.

After leaving ZAMCOM in 2013, I joined Limelight Photography, a subsidiary of Tronix Zambia Limited. I managed the company, did photography and attended to clients. And in February 2014, I joined the 'prestigious' Post Newspapers Zambia Limited (in liquidation) as a photojournalist.

You may be wondering why I'm sharing all this information. Well, this was the sequence of events that laid the foundation for the events I experienced over the years as a photojournalist. Without further ado, let's fuse in the story....

They asked why I was taking pictures and what media organisation I was representing. Clad in US Marine-type uniforms and wearing green berets, they folded their sleeves and flexed their muscles as they advanced towards me.

Consumed by fear, I retreated as they approached. As I did so, I felt somebody stand behind me. Alas, It was one of them. He too asked me why I had taken pictures of them doing what they were doing and which media house I was representing.

I told them I was working for the *Zambia News and Information Services (ZANIS)*. One of them reached for my pockets for an identity card but did not find any. Even the overzealous youth standing couldn't trace where I had hidden my Post identity card.

CHAPTER ONE

I told them I worked for ZANIS with the hope of being let loose of their web. I was afraid to mention I was from *The Post*, afraid that they were going to 'kill me'. They had stones in their hands.

They found it difficult to believe I was from '*ZANIS*'. They grabbed me by the belt, roughed me up and stole my two cell phones from my pockets. They also got away with a wallet containing some money, my National Registration Card and voter's card, among other personal documents.

They dragged me to a drain near the Seventh Day Adventist Church on Lusaka's Independence Avenue as if I were a condemned criminal. They lifted me and tossed me into the muddy waters, taking turns at beating me while I firmly held on to my Canon 650D camera which had pictures of them burning regalia belonging to the opposition United Party for National Development (UPND).

I had captured pictures of the suspected Patriotic Front (PF) cadres overpowering youths clad in UPND regalia, that had thronged the Freedom Statue to commemorate the 2016 Youth Day. Despite my best efforts to protect the camera, the incensed youths damaged it deliberately.

As I take you through this brutal journalism experience in my country Zambia, a quick look at events that led to where I am today will suffice.

In Zambia, enrolling to study journalism is exciting to the applicant, but to others it signals signing one's own 'death sentence'! However, this notion is reliant on what kind of journalism you branch into and decide to practice after graduation.

I must state here that those that branch into investigative journalism—'critical reporting' face the greatest threat of political harassment and police intimidation. On the other end of this spectrum, those that practice under public media and only highlight 'developmental programmes' for the government have less chances of being harassed and are often regarded as "ethical", "hard working" and "professional" scribes by those they report about.

In short, scribes from the public media are somewhat safe. And those from the private media are the prey.

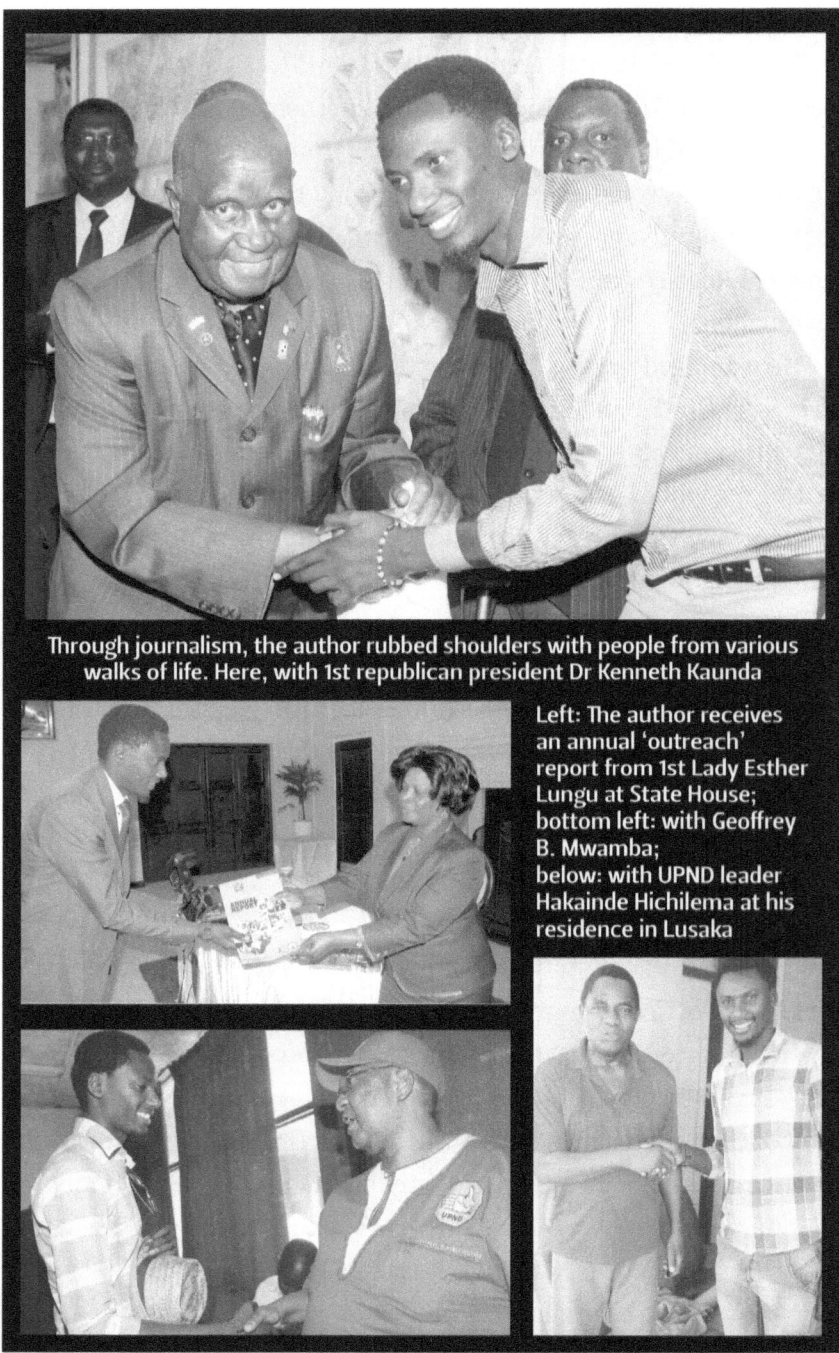

Through journalism, the author rubbed shoulders with people from various walks of life. Here, with 1st republican president Dr Kenneth Kaunda

Left: The author receives an annual 'outreach' report from 1st Lady Esther Lungu at State House; bottom left: with Geoffrey B. Mwamba; below: with UPND leader Hakainde Hichilema at his residence in Lusaka

CHAPTER ONE

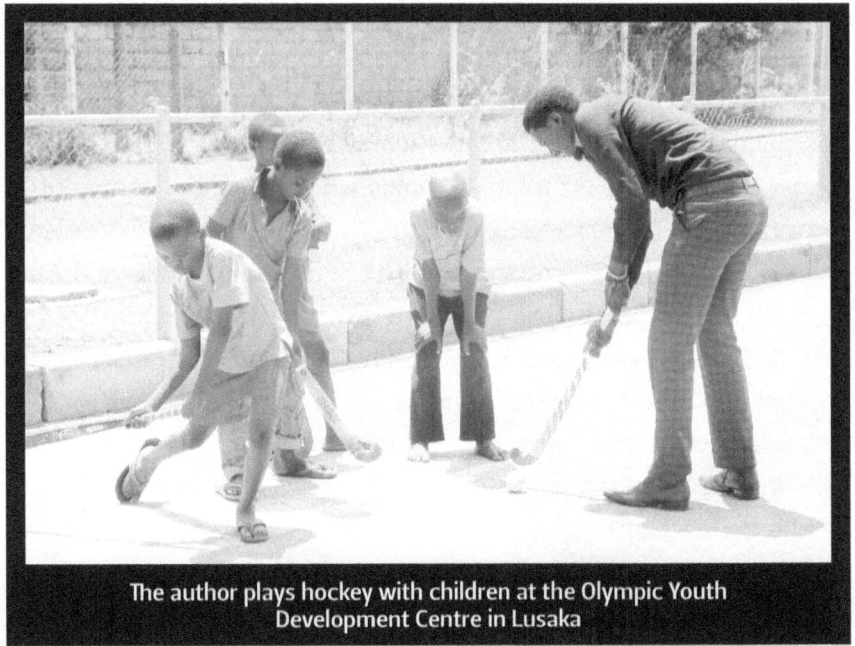
The author plays hockey with children at the Olympic Youth Development Centre in Lusaka

However, the journalism arena has in the recent past turned out to be almost comical in the sense that journalists from both the public and private media have accepted a trend where they take each other on, thereby becoming rivals in the profession.

But in whose interests do they wage these fights against each other? Let's highlight some issues regarding the growing tension between both sectors.

Almost everyone privy to this information will attest that journalists have had unlimited access to all sorts of personalities in society since time immemorial. This access ranges from a street vendor to the presidency. And they enjoy this access to the point of abusing it, thus merely becoming advertising agents for self-centred politicians in exchange for freebies and jobs, among other benefits.

When this is unfolding, journalists abandon reporting on issues of national interest—that is matters that affect the ordinary person—and tend to prioritise that which is to their convenience—that which impresses their paymasters.

2016, and perhaps even previous years, have had the clearest indications of what I can loosely define as 'cadre journalism'.

Journalists consciously and unconsciously become political 'cadres'. I say unconsciously because in the course of discharging public relations for political party A as directed by media house owners in pursuit of the attainment of the so-called agendas, such journalists, before they realise it, would have turned out to be more hardened cadres of the institutions they report for than the owners themselves. And consciously, they do it for personal interests to receive favours from the politician.

Today, journalists have colleagues in the media fraternity whom they perceive as enemies because of their differences in political ideologies and varying agendas, among all sorts of excuses they might put up to defend their actions.

Now, while at ZAMCOM, my course-mates (Oscar Malipenga, Mark Ziligone, Abel Phiri, Derrick Silimina among other) and I would often discuss politics and media freedoms with the use of newspapers as reference aids. Often we'd ask each other which media outlet we would choose to work for, given the opportunity. Several of my friends chose the *Zambia National Broadcasting Corporation (ZNBC)*, while others picked the privately-owned Muvi Television. I would pick the *Zambia Daily Mail*.

I had heard many stories about *The Post*, then, the country's largest selling privately-owned newspaper. Stories topping the list were that the proprietor and editor-In-chief of this newspaper, Fred M'membe led a life of luxury while he 'failed' to pay his employees' salaries.

Also stories of how tough *The Post* newsroom was, were prominent among issues surrounding this critical newspaper. Against this background, I never at any instance ever dreamed of setting foot in the company, whether on industrial attachment or employment basis. I thus ended up doing my internship with the *Zambia Daily Mail* in 2013.

When I completed my journalism studies later that year, I worked for Limelight Photography from December that year to the following February when I garnered courage and faced my fears.

CHAPTER ONE

We had heard that *The Post* newsroom was as hot as the surface of a running car engine. And even though we heard that the story/idea presentation during the early morning diary meetings were no easy undertaking for scribes that worked there, we somewhat downplayed it. But this had become the time to garner strength and fanaticism to work for this critical privately-owned newspaper.

Incredibly, when I saw an advert where *The Post* sought to recruit a photojournalist, I applied without hesitation.

My very first day at the Post was electric. I saw what many people were scared of. Indeed, idea presentation in that newsroom was quite daunting, particularly for someone new as I was. It was very difficult, but it was clearly attainable to those that were determined to succeed. The newsroom environment came with challenges; some so unbearable that there were journalists who would leave at the end of the day and never to return. *The Post* demanded critical thinking amongst its workers, an excellent quality I associate with M'membe.

So my first opportunity to prove that I was capable of standing these pressures was soon to come.

Every morning, usually at 08:00hours, most media houses have planning meetings, otherwise known as 'diary meetings'. During these meetings, journalists present stories they may have lined up to be considered for publication or broadcast for that day or the following day's edition. Also conducted during these meetings, in the case of newspapers, are reviews of that day's edition.

It was my first day in *The Post* newsroom diary meeting. Before the meeting commenced, Bivan Saluseki, managing editor at the time, introduced me to fellow journalists that had sat around an oval-like table. Everyone loosened up and allowed a polite smile to cross their faces and welcomed me to *The Post* and to the diary meeting.

The meeting began with a reviewing of that day's newspaper edition. Then each person was given an opportunity to present three introductions to their story and picture ideas. The ideas had to be workable. The environment became more and more intimidating when I observed and heard people's ideas being shot down. In my heart, I said, "tomorrow, I will feign illness". I felt it was already too much for me to bear. And this was just my first day!

My turn came. I presented my three ideas, two of which were almost immediately struck down. That day, the editors encouraged me to begin working in advance and on the need to strengthen my news judgment ability.

With time, I learned the art of idea generation and how to defend my proposals when they were challenged. The fear left, and ultimately, I was on top of my game. But my practice was not perfect, I recall making a mistake in a caption thereby forcing the newspaper to carry an apology in the following day's edition. One thing I learnt after making an error is that, mistakes cost media houses both money and reputation. This taught me to be accurate when dealing with information.

It is important to note here that at the time I was joining the newspaper, the President of the Republic was Michael Chilufya Sata, who enjoyed unenviably favourable coverage with *The Post*.

We were the most admired and respected (some would even say feared) newspaper in the country. Government officials, ruling and opposition party supporters, the police, among other citizens, admired the paper. It seemed as though everyone wanted to work with us, for some reason. Colleagues from various media outlets envied us. They wished they could work for this paper but many of them were a little scared of the 'hostile' newsroom and diary meetings.

The Post newspaper had the most attractive pay for its employees, among Zambia's private media houses, and some people would remark, '*The Post* pays its journalists mad salaries'. And indeed, Post employees' salaries were among the best in the local media industry.

Flying with the Scotts

"Line up and wait, hold short delta, runway two-seven, radar contact…" Those were the words I recall echoing as aircraft controllers

CHAPTER ONE

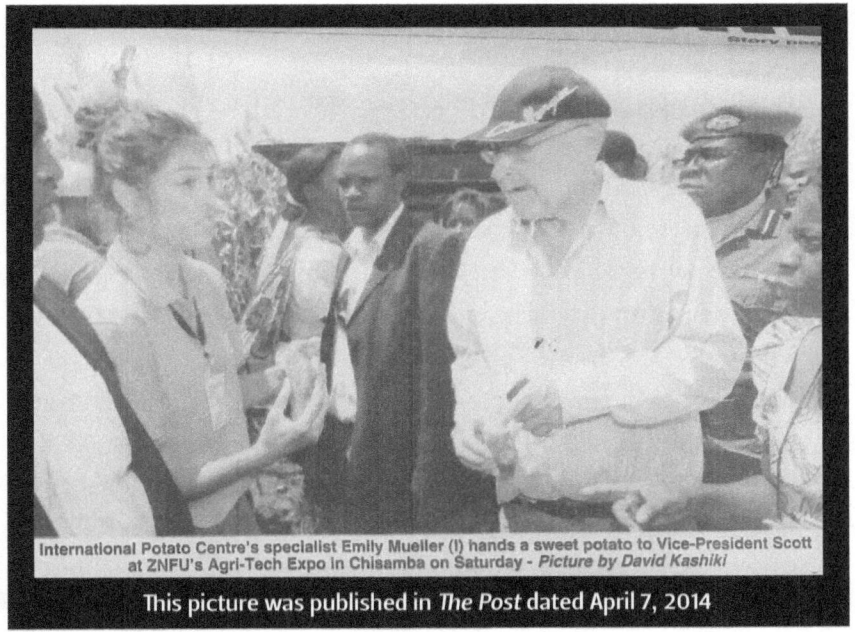

International Potato Centre's specialist Emily Mueller (l) hands a sweet potato to Vice-President Scott at ZNFU's Agri-Tech Expo in Chisamba on Saturday - *Picture by David Kashiki*

This picture was published in *The Post* dated April 7, 2014

communicated with the two pilots in the helicopter that flew Vice-President Dr Guy Scott, his wife Charlotte and myself back to Lusaka from Chisamba.

Every year, The Zambia National Farmers' Union holds an Agritech Expo at the Golden valley Agricultural Research Trust (GART) in Chisamba where local and international exhibitors showcase their farming equipment, livestock and crops. The April 2014 expo was officiated by Dr Scott, then Zambia's Republican Vice-President. Apart from being the country's first—and so far, only—white vice-president, Dr Scott was himself a farmer and had even once served as agriculture minister.

As he went around the stands, Dr Scott stopped at one to chew raw orange-sweet potatoes handed to him by an exhibitor.

This characteristically 'Zambian' gesture by the Vice-President captivated exhibitors and clients alike. Dr Scott was always easy-going and his carefree demeanour endeared him to many people.

Officially launching the 2014 Expo, Dr Scott declined to read the speech that had been prepared for him. "Written speeches are boring," he said. "Jokes are written for me. I have my own jokes I would want to tell. And worse, they write me same jokes everywhere I address people".

He added that he could not follow the speech because many things written in speeches were hollow and empty statements that many people did not take seriously. This brought laughter to attendees at the event.

Being a photojournalist from The Post at that time was a great privilege. And covering the event in 2014 'earned' me a lift on the chopper, allowing me to rub shoulders with the second most powerful couple in the country.

During the event, whenever Dr Scott wanted to make a comment, he would look around to see if Post journalists were nearby. He had trust in the newspaper and described its journalists as "the most accurate and factual scribes to have ever covered me." Moses Kuwema was seemingly the Vice-President's favourite reporter, one whom he could 'not' go anywhere without.

We were admired by many because of how the PF government under Michael Sata treated us. Everyone respected us. The 2014 Agritech Expo launch proceeded well and was a success.

It was soon time for his honour the Vice-President and Dr Charlotte Scott to leave.

Officials lined up near the helicopter to bid farewell to the vice-president who had to return to Lusaka for other duties. Clad in brown farmers' outfits, the Scotts shook hands with exhibitors and the event organisers and boarded the aircraft. I was in the media tent at the time, copying pictures from my camera and emailing them back to the office for the following day's edition. I worked feverishly, trying to beat the deadline.

Suddenly, one of Dr Scott's security men burst into the tent. "Kashiki," he said, his brow bristling with sweat. "Let's go. The Vice-President is waiting for you." I nearly jumped out of my skin, my eyes almost popping out of their sockets. I asked the man if he was joking, but the look on his face made it clear that he was not. Apparently, Dr Scott had delayed take-off and ordered his security detail to look for me. He wanted me to join him on the flight back to Lusaka. The security aide quickly helped me pack my equipment, lifted my bag, and we both rushed towards the chopper.

The aide's name was Martin Mwewa-Mukobeka, a police officer whom I had come to know while covering Dr Scott on assignments.

As we approached the helicopter, another security officer popped out and rushed me aboard. I was more than nervous, but Dr Charlotte Scott put me at ease, inviting me to take a seat between herself and her husband. The gesture left me gob-smacked. It was a surreal moment, aboard a helicopter with the second most powerful couple in the country!

The Scotts helped me fasten my seatbelt, a gesture that also thrilled me. "What happened to you the first time you got on a chopper?" Dr Charlotte asked with a chuckle. "Some people vomit you know, but let's hope it's not your first."

Dr Scott and I laughed. The chopper slowly lifted off, and I was happy that I wasn't experiencing the nausea I expected.

Flying with the Scotts was a thrilling and unforgettable experience, and I must state that I learnt so much about the Vice-President.

En route to their residence in Lusaka's lush New Kasama area, the Scotts bided the time with anecdotes as we flew over the greenery, slums and beautiful sites the city has to offer.

I must confess that understanding Vice-President Scott's jokes while on the chopper demanded one being very attentive. Dr Scott's voice is naturally soft, with an unmistakable English accent punctuated by quips in the local vernacular languages. Most of his jokes actually went over my head, but I politely laughed along while marvelling at the awesome view outside.

As we approached the Vice-President's residence, they asked if I had enjoyed flying with them and I responded in the affirmative. They too were happy, especially that I did not throw up!

Immediately after we touched down that afternoon, Mukobeka handed me my bag, and one of the drivers in Dr Scott's motorcade drove me straight to *The Post* offices on Bwinjimfumu Road.

No picture was worth my life

Whatever goes up, it is said, must surely come down. *The Post*'s fall from grace began shortly after the death of President Sata. However, some say, the fall of the Post started as far back as 2004, a time the newspaper was alleged to have stated courting the Levy Mwanawasa led government. But, the 'eventual' fall came about after my newspaper took a stance against the PF's choice for Sata's successor, Edgar Chagwa Lungu. *The Post* reported that Mr Lungu had no capacity to rule, and that as a lawyer, he once 'embezzled' a client's legal fees and had failed effectively to discharge services.

During a Radio Phoenix Let the People Talk programme of December 5, 2014, Lungu himself told the nation that he had "no vision" for the remaining period following President Sata's demise. And also, Mr Lungu said he would instead continue implementing his predecessor's vision. The media reported that he literary had no vision, but, he argued that the context in which he remarked that, was misinterpreted.

Covering political events during President Sata's tenure was even easier if you came from *The Post* than it was for those from the public media. *The Post* had pictures and stories that the public media could not have. *The Post* had easy access to the PF government under the stewardship of Mr Sata.

President Sata died in a London hospital on October 28, 2014. For the second time in its history, Zambia began preparing for elections following the death of a President in office.

And so when then PF presidential candidate Edgar Lungu hit the campaign trail, because of the 'negative' coverage he got from *The Post*, he and sympathisers made it clear that they were in a tussle with Post proprietor Fred M'membe who was believed to not have wanted Lungu to pull through in the January 2015 presidential elections. So, Lungu started the tussle promising Zambians that once given the mandate,

CHAPTER ONE

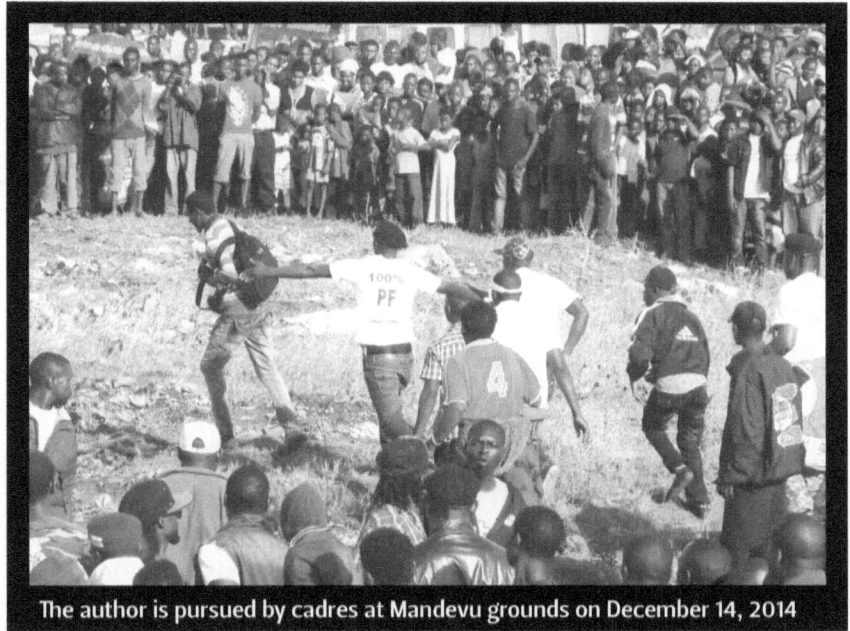

The author is pursued by cadres at Mandevu grounds on December 14, 2014

his government would collect debt from tax defaulting companies with an indirect reference to *The Post*.

"There is a media house that does not want me to go to State House. They are painting me as unreliable, a rogue and so on and so forth. They did the same thing to President Sata; they called him names and they turned around and claimed he was their darling. Just wait, they will turn around and come to me," Lungu said on Radio Phoenix in December 2014.

This marked the beginning of the conflict between the two. Usually, in the field when covering events, those with cameras and recorders are easily identified as journalists. And so if you represent a media house that a particular political party is in bad standing with, you would easily be identified and hounded out, or worse still, assaulted.

Lungu held a campaign rally in Lusaka's Mandevu Township on December 14, 2014 after touring most parts of the country, and I was tasked to cover it.

To this day, chills still run down my spine when I recall the events of that day. I try hard not to think about it, but for the purpose of posterity, I will share it here.

In the company of then Post journalist Roy Habaalu and photojournalist Tobias Phiri, I arrived at the Mandevu grounds where Lungu was to campaign. While walking to the spot where a stage had been set up, I whispered jokingly in Habaalu's ear, "You will be beaten by the PF cadres". We laughed about it, and brushed it off like the awkward joke it was. But it wasn't.

It was around 16:00 hours, when the PF's choice for 2015 presidential by-elections, Edgar Lungu, dressed in a black corduroy suit and white shirt took to the stage, flashed the party symbol of a clenched fist and chanted the PF slogan. His supporters responded with raised clenched fists.

While this was happening, Tobias and I had already positioned ourselves near the stage in order to get the best shots. Tobias was on top of the large speakers, while I and colleagues from other media houses stood at the front of the stage where Lungu and PF officials were standing addressing scores of supporters.

I had just taken a few 'shots' of Lungu when I felt a tap on my shoulder. I quickly turned to see a young muscular man clad in a T-shirt inscribed with the words "100% PF". Before I could say a thing, he asked—in fact, ordered—me to follow him. Struck with fear, I told him in a shaky voice that I was busy. I said I was working and that I could not leave the spot I was in and asked him to tell me what he wanted from me.

While Lungu delivered his speech on stage, this guy became physical. He grabbed me by the belt and with the help of another well-built up youth, pulled me through the crowd that had gathered to listen to the PF presidential candidate. They asked me where I was from. I told them I was reporting for the Zambia News and Information Services (ZANIS). They then asked for my identity card. I told them I had left it at the office. They were clearly not convinced.

As they dragged me through the crowd, the duo repeatedly punched

CHAPTER ONE

me in the chest and ribs. As we reached the far end of the crowds, I panicked and remembered that I was dealing with people who knew who I was and the media house I was reporting for. So I removed my Canon Speedlite 600EX II-RT Flash from the camera shoe, packed it and the camera in the black backpack, as the horde of suspected cadres grew and surrounded me while people just watched.

To avoid creating a scene at the Mandevu grounds, the youths asked me to run like I was escaping from Sobibor, so they could chase after me. And if I was caught, I'd be sorted out away from the sight of the crowd. They had clearly watched too many movies. I hit the ground running as they tried in vain to keep up with me. How I lost them and where I was, I can not recall, but all I recollect is hailing a bus that was heading into town and getting on it.

Little did I know that, while this was going on, Tobias was photographing the whole scene from his vantage point on top of the huge speakers. He too could have been noticed, but he courageously took the pictures with his telephoto Canon 70-200mm lens on a 650D cannon camera series. He couldn't come to my aid as he too would have been hounded. Most likely his equipment would have been destroyed by the suspected PF cadres. And so, he did well. I took one for the team.

On the bus, I received a call from Tobias. He had trailed me for about 10 minutes after he saw me running. He said the company car was ready to take us to safety. I alighted from the bus, and a Post vehicle arrived to pick me. We drove away from Mandevu without uttering a word. I was traumatised.

After we arrived at *The Post* newspapers offices on the famous Bwinjimfumu Road around 18:00 hours, I rushed to inform my news editor Joseph Mwenda about the incident. He arranged for me to be taken to hospital that evening. Pictures of me being harassed by youths clad in PF regalia and my running away from them were published in *The Post* edition of December 15, 2014. My persecution by suspected PF cadres was frightening, and became a topic almost everyone expressed concern and joked about. It would, however, not be the last.

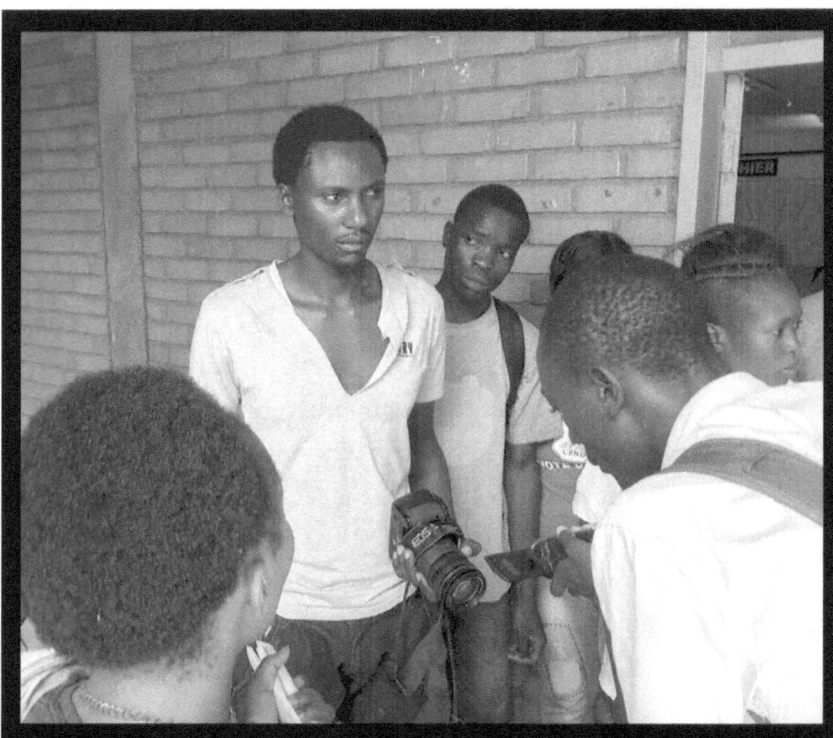

Being interviewed by fellow journalists at University Teaching Hospital after an attack during youth day celebrations March 12, 2016

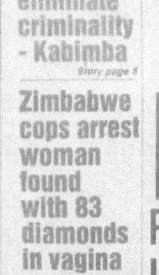

The Post edition of March 13, 2016

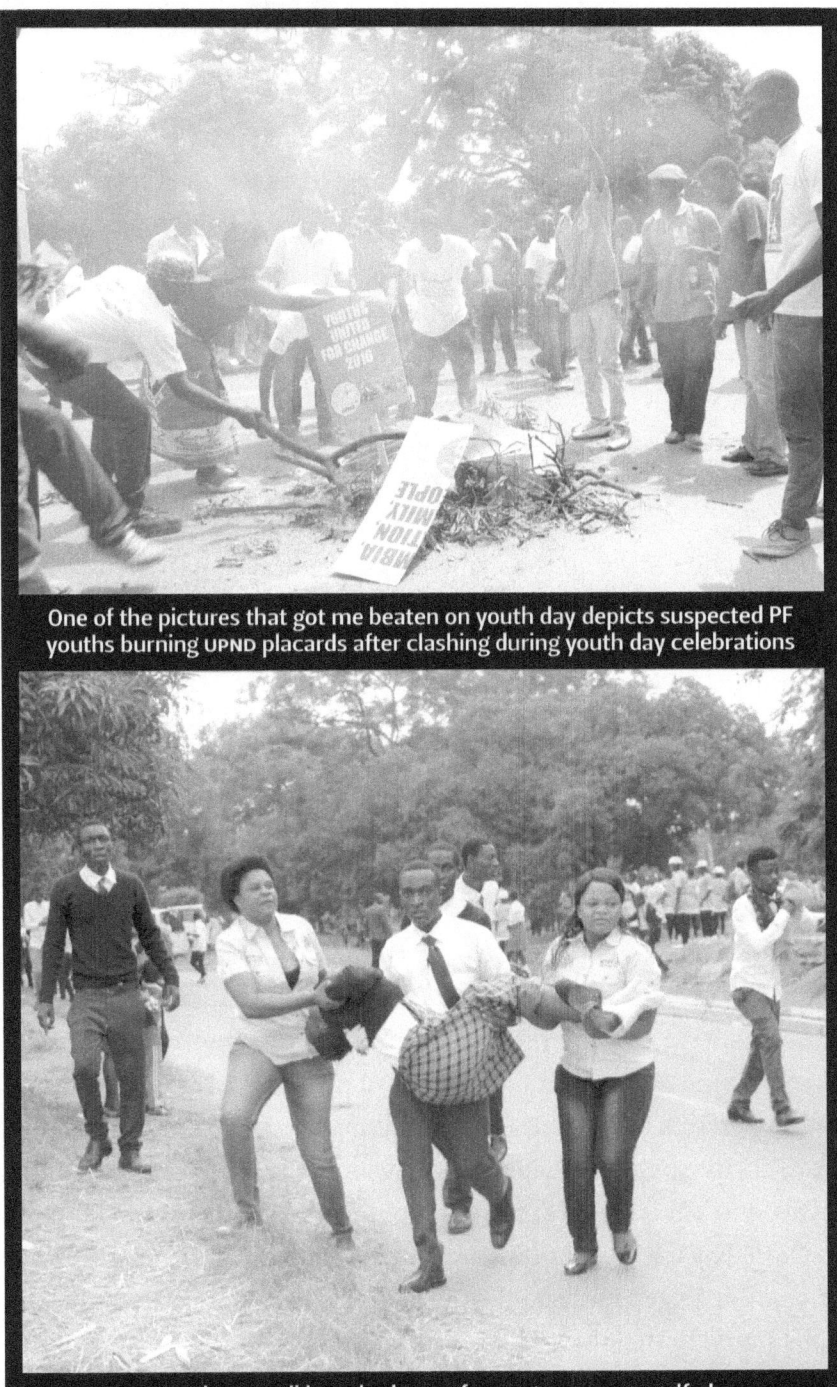

One of the pictures that got me beaten on youth day depicts suspected PF youths burning UPND placards after clashing during youth day celebrations

An unconscious pupil is rushed away from a tear-gas engulfed area

My 'bloody 2016 Youth Day present'

Somewhere they read that I had been assaulted, and that my attackers had gotten away with all my personal belongings. They were glued to social media to know how I was doing. They were gravely worried about me. I had no phone to contact and tell them how I was attacked. So they contacted almost everyone they could to get information about how I was doing—my family was unease.

Shunning public events, non-issue-based criticism and irrelevant politicking at the expense of discussing fuel prices, better social services and reducing the ever-widening gap between the poor and the rich can well be associated with Zambian politics.

During Youth Day celebrations, independence anniversaries and other public events on the Zambian and international calendar, the opposition political parties air their grievances by shunning such events as a way of sending a message of displeasure on how citizens' affairs are (mis)managed by the ruling party.

Every year, Youth Day is marked by scores of young people from schools, colleges, political parties and institutions undertaking marches across the country. Typically, the marches are held in the morning and end with speeches from government officials as well as representatives from youth groups.

But 2016 was a different year for the opposition and the ruling Patriotic Front (PF). The 2016 Youth Day commemorations on March 12 in Lusaka were graced by Republican Vice-President Inonge Wina.

At around 08:30 hours, hundreds of pupils, the differently-abled and majorettes had already started taking up their slots in readiness for the march past on Independence Avenue which began at the Lusaka Civic Centre and ended at the Freedom Statue where they were to be addressed by the Vice-President. Youths believed to be from the opposition UPND joined the festivities in good time and took up the marching slot allotted to them by the event organisers.

Arriving in hundreds a few minutes before the start of the procession were youths clad in PF regalia. The energetic 'PF' youths arrived at the venue several minutes after their 'UPND' counterparts. However, after noticing that the UPND youths were going to march in front of them, the PF confronted their counterparts who also did not take this lightly.

A fight ensued.

Riot police attempted to disperse the fighting youths by firing tear gas. The result left hundreds of pupils and other participants choking, with some even becoming unconscious. Some pupils were rushed away from the scene by their brave colleagues. The ensuing chaos at this event resembled the end of an action movie.

All this was unfolding outside the Seventh Adventist Church on Independence Avenue—roughly 300 metres from the Freedom Statue where Vice-President Wina was awaiting the marchers.

Noticing the mayhem, I and Isaac Nsoneka, a colleague from Pan African Radio, dashed to the scene with the hope of getting first-hand information on what was going on.

Carried away with taking pictures of the fight among the police, and two political youth camps, I discovered that Nsoneka was nowhere to be seen. I continued documenting this fracas which left many UPND youths in need of medical treatment.

These pictures were going to be front page pictures for my critical newspaper. *The Post* newspaper often carried most controversial pictures on its front page. And the confusion at an event like the Youth Day was news that I as a photojournalist could not ignore.

Anyhow, before I could realise that it was getting too dangerous, the suspected PF youths that were burning UPND regalia noticed me taking pictures. One of them demanded that I hand over the camera, but I declined and took several steps back. I bumped into a horde of incensed 'cadres' that immediately held me.

They asked why I was taking pictures, and what media organisation I was representing. Gripped by fear, I did not respond and instead looked around for an escape route.

Clad in PF party regalia, United States' Marine-like uniforms, and wearing green berets, some cadres folded their sleeves and flexed their muscles as they charged towards me. I tried again to escape but their colleagues only tightened their grip on my arms.

One of them asked me again why I had taken pictures of them doing what they were doing, and which media house in particular I was coming from. I again told them I was working for ZANIS. But they too were sceptical; so one of them reached for my pockets to check for a ZANIS identity card.

One huge muscular individual searched my pockets, but did not find any ID, not even my Post identity card that was hidden in another pocket.

Knowing how critical my newspaper was towards government, and some individuals, I told them I worked for ZANIS with a hope of being let loose of their web. I was afraid to mention I was from The Post; they were going to sort me out.

Unconvinced that I was from ZANIS, they grabbed me by the belt, roughed me up and stole my two cell phones. They also got away with a wallet containing a few 'kwachas', my National Registration Card and my Voter's Card.

Then they dragged me to a drain near the Seventh Day Adventist Church, punching me repeatedly before tossing me into its muddy waters. As they embarrassingly beat the life out of me, I held firmly on to my camera which had pictures of them burning UPND regalia.

They started dragging me to 'their boss'. "*Timupeleke che kuli ba* boss, *niwaku* Post *uyu nimuziba* ('let's just take him to the boss, I know this guy, he is from *The Post*'," one said. "He wants to show that our party is violent."

"If I get to their boss, I will die," I thought to myself quietly, "these people are ruthless." Then, after failing to agree on whether to take me to their "boss" or sort me out themselves proved difficult, their attention drifted. At this point, one of them asked me to run. As I mentioned earlier, these youths seem to watch too many action movies.

I heeded his advice and ran for my life. Fortunately, I saw a police officer who was approaching the place of the confusion. Seeing me with a police officer, the incensed youths hastily retreated and I jumped on a taxi despite not having any money.

The taxi driver looked surprised; he seemingly didn't want to ask me too many questions seeing how muddied I was, with tattered clothes. His only question was, "Where do I take you?" With a faint voice, I replied "Mobi Television" fearful that he might be one of the suspected PF youths; and that, by mentioning that I was going to *The Post*, I would have placed myself in more danger. At that time, Mobi Television was situated next to Post Newspapers.

When we reached Mobi TV, I felt a bit comfortable and told him my destination was *The Post*, and we parked inside the company's premises.

I walked into the newsroom, my eyes filled with mud and tears. I opened the door to news-editor Joseph Mwenda's office, he was not there. I walked to the main newsroom where I found my colleagues there, who reacted with shock looking at my appearance. I asked whether they had seen Mwenda around, but none of them answered me, numbed with shock. So I walked over to the assistant editor Masuzyo Chakwe's office, where I found Mwenda. Both their jaws dropped.

Walking me back to his office, Mwenda asked whether I had been in an accident that Saturday afternoon. I told him people in PF regalia had attacked me while I was taking pictures of the confusion at the Youth Day celebrations. I told him all of my belongings had been stolen, and that the only thing I managed to secure was the camera which the cadres had broken.

When Fred M'membe walked in, and saw my condition, he asked Mwenda what had happened to me. As Mwenda briefed him, I sat quietly, barely hearing what was being said.

After about 15 minutes of debriefing, we realised that the taxi driver was still waiting, so Mwenda went outside and paid him.

The company through Mwenda, immediately rushed me to the University Teaching Hospital (UTH) where I was examined, treated and given a medical report highlighting a bruised eyeball, internal injuries and general body pains. While at the UTH, I met several other youths at the casualty section clad in 'bloody' UPND regalia. They too seemed to have been in grave pain.

From the hospital, Mwenda drove me to Lusaka Central Police Station to report the matter. As an officer recorded a statement from me, Mwenda took pictures. But as he did so, four riot police officers walked in and demanded that he stop taking pictures at the station.

He tried to explain his reasons for taking the pictures but they dragged him out of the interview room and ordered him to delete the pictures, threatening to deal with him if he didn't do so.

Instead of sympathising with me who had been attacked, the officers then walked to where I was standing while giving a statement to the officer on duty and attempted to drag me outside the station saying I was the reason Mwenda took pictures at a police station and demanded that I leave.

I almost vented my anger on the police officers who had no sense of empathy towards me in my difficult moment. They confiscated Mwenda's camera and gave it to a senior police officer. And fortunately, when this senior police officer saw me in the images in the camera, he walked downstairs and found me in a tussle with his subordinates. Upon seeing him, the cops froze and saluted.

He asked them why they behaved the way that they did. But without an explanation, they apologised to him. Pointing at me, he told them, "This is my young man, he is a journalist, let's work with journalists, they are our partners." That's how the issue was resolved and we had a police report that yielded nothing at all after a spirited tussle with cops. I guess that was my 'special' Youth Day mayhem present.

The bullet that sent Post Journalists running

Shortly after assistant news editor Masuzyo Chakwe had walked through a corridor en route to the newsroom at *The Post* offices, a bullet pierced the newsroom and landed in the same passage. CCTV footage

CHAPTER ONE

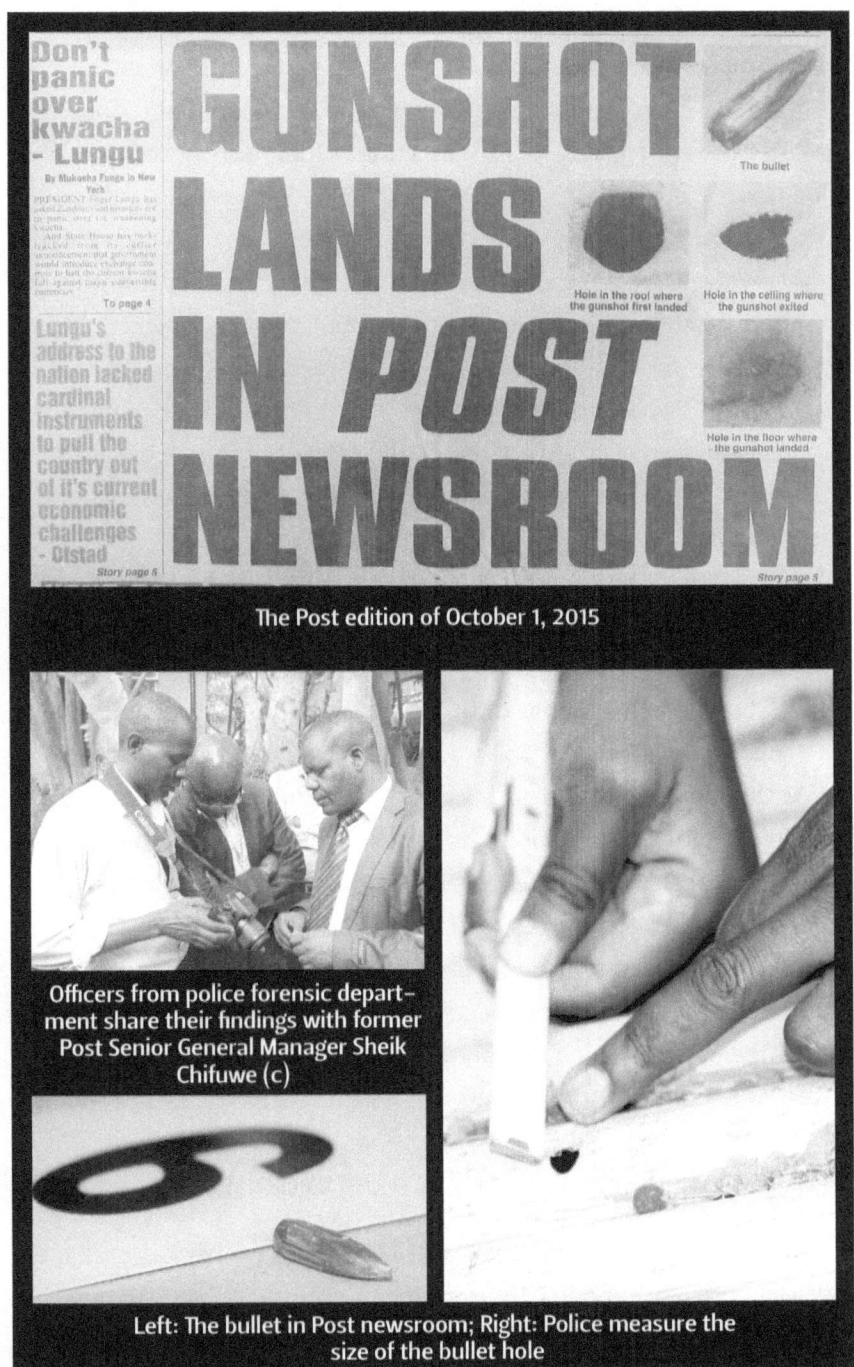

The Post edition of October 1, 2015

Officers from police forensic department share their findings with former Post Senior General Manager Sheik Chifuwe (c)

Left: The bullet in Post newsroom; Right: Police measure the size of the bullet hole

revealed that this happened around 12:30 hours on September 30, 2015, approximately 2 minutes after Chakwe had walked the passage.

The Post newspapers had two newsrooms, a large one housing a majority of reporters, and a smaller one which only accommodated about four.

On that eventful September day, work was proceeding normally and we were preparing copy for the following day's edition. Other members of staff were proceeding to the staff canteen for lunch. It was a normal day. That is, until a loud scream punctuated the air. Kombe Mataka, a reporter who worked at a desk in the smaller newsroom, had heard a loud bang and got up to investigate the source of the noise. She peeped into the corridor and upon seeing a bullet on the floor, let out a loud shout.

We rushed to see what had made her scream. Unable to say a word, she just pointed at the bullet on the floor. It was just over a metre away from her seat. Alarmed, we thought the shooter may have been in the ceiling. So, quickly, people among them Fred M'membe, gathered at the scene.

At this point, our editor-In-chief, M'membe advised us to leave the offices, which we all did, while police were called in. They arrived about 20 minutes later to assess where the bullet which had pierced the rooftop and newsroom had come from.

As plain clothed police officers from the forensic department examined the scene, workers speculated that the shooter was targeting M'membe's office which was about four metres away from where the bullet had landed.

Police at 'war' with UPND cadres

Working outside our closed Post Newspapers offices in Lusaka, we saw a van full of riot police drive down Bwinjimfumu Road. Wondering what was going on and where the officers were heading, I received a call that police had just arrived at the UPND secretariat on Provident Street

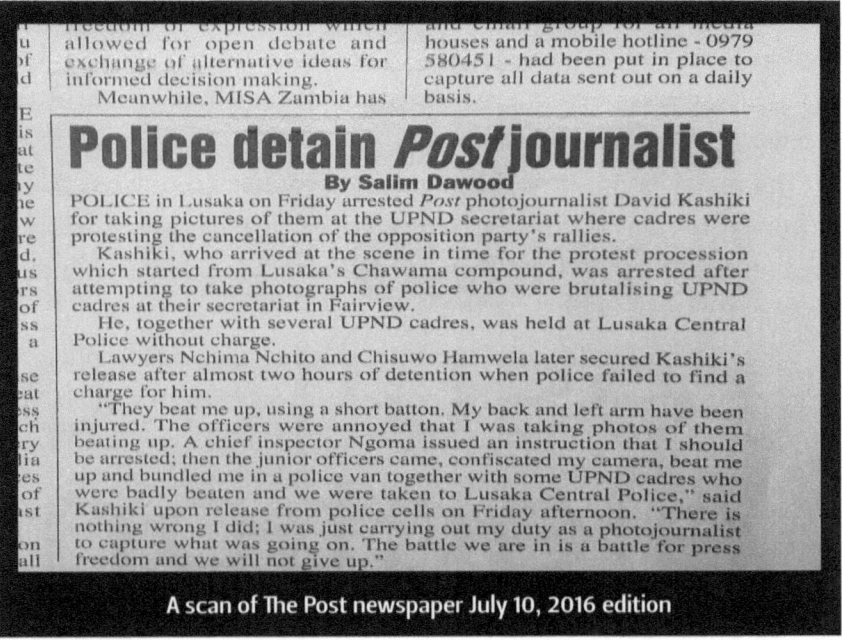

A scan of The Post newspaper July 10, 2016 edition

in Fairview area and that people there were being arrested.

I immediately headed there and when I arrived outside the secretariat, a number of people, including women who sold roasted groundnuts nearby as well as children playing social football on this road, had all been apprehended and bundled into a police van.

Shortly before this operation at the secretariat, police and UPND cadres had clashed on Kafue Road, resulting in the shooting to death of a female youth, Mapenzi Chibulo. The clash occurred after police decided to cancel a permit for a political rally that the UPND had planned for Chawama compound in Lusaka.

The cancellation came a few hours if not less, before the rally was scheduled to begin, angering scores of UPND supporters who had already gathered there, and those en route. The angry supporters marched in protest against the decision and insisted on proceeding with the rally.

Upon hearing this, the police command deployed officers to quell the unfolding scenario which had begun to inconvenience motorists and cause traffic jams. In the ensuing melee, Mapenzi was shot dead by one police officer. This agitated the hundreds of supporters who later fought running battles with the police. Word soon went round that police officers were overwhelmed and ruthlessly clobbered by the incensed UPND youths!

You may wonder how this incident is connected to what police officers were doing at the UPND secretariat. Well, police suspected that the UPND cadres that 'beat' them up on Kafue Road went into hiding at the party secretariat.

So, as I arrived at the secretariat, I greeted several senior police officers who were already there and proceeded to take pictures. But before long, one officer ordered his subordinates to confiscate my camera and put me on the van.

The over-excited officers swiftly swung into action, hitting me with their batons and kicking me as though I was a victim of mob justice. I was thrown into the van which was already full and immediately sped off to Lusaka Central Police Station. Arriving there, we were made to sit on wet ground.

The officers were still mad that I had taken pictures of them 'brutally' arresting UPND youths that 'beat them up' on Kafue Road. So, when they made me sit on the wet ground, some took turns slapping and kicking me.

"What did you want to do with those pictures *iwe kambwanga* [you fool]?" they bellowed. I was defenceless; they beat me while others watched. This was only halted by one senior officer who said, "You have already done a good job, so let us not overstep our boundaries *bashilikale*[soldiers]". With that, they stopped beating me.

Battered and sitting on the police station's wet ground among the UPND cadres, I pulled my phone out of my pockets and called news-editor Joseph Mwenda to tell him I was in trouble. He hastily informed our company lawyers who, together with him, rushed to the police station on Church Road, where they found that I had already been put behind bars.

I was released from police cells around 16:00hours, about three hours after I had been detained. On releasing me from police custody, a senior officer told his subordinates that journalists were not to be apprehended if they were only carrying out their duties. The senior officer came to the holding cell in the company of lawyers from Nchito and Nchito Advocates.

During those brief hours in detention, I heard a lot of stories that, up to now, make sense. One man, the cell captain, asked me about the political situation outside detention.

I explained a few things to them, and the captain told me what he thought about what was going on. "You know, these politicians are useless, they use innocent women and children to gain votes. And never at one time have they used their own children to fight political battles for them, that's why *ni anyandule*," he said.

"The police are used to brutalise their brothers and sisters—the people they suffer together with—because of selfish politicians. It's sad for them too, the police are also victims of injustices perpetrated by politicians and we must not hate them. We are all victims of unjust individuals".

I agreed with him and reflected on his thoughts. My conclusion was that, his thoughts needed to be shared.

It's, however, saddening to state that even innocent women and children were among those detained. But fortunately, they were later released following the intervention of legal counsels from the UPND.

Nonetheless, I believe that Zambia can be rebuilt and the police can treat innocent people with the dignity and respect they deserve. It's worth noting that the police too, are victims of a selfish some politician's motives and injustices. They need support from all of us and every citizen must accept and help them discharge their duties professionally. Not all police officers are unprofessional; I personally have good relations with some officers, who somewhat made my work even easier while documenting events in hostile environments.

So, that's how I was jointly brutalised with 'supporters' of the UPND in July 2016. And when they handed me back my camera, the images

I had taken of them beating women and cadres had all been deleted.

The Board of the World Association of Newspapers and News Publishers (WAN-IFRA), met in Durban, South Africa on June 7, 2017, where they called for renewed global solidarity with the Zambian press in the wake of attacks and the hardening government stance against independent, free media.

Below are excerpts from the report: *"...The Board notes with concern the questioning of Prime TV managing director Gerald Shawa and station manager Makokwa Kozi over a letter sent by police demanding the station hand over footage from an opposition briefing. The Board further condemns the April 2017 beating and brief detention by police of journalists Alex Musokotwane of Muvi TV and Kalan Muchima of Prime TV while at an opposition leader's home. Zambian authorities' efforts to intimidate journalists for reporting opposition voices are inconsistent with the principles of press freedom....*

...The Board notes with concern the July 2016 arrest of David Kashiki, photographer for The Post, as he attempted to take pictures of suspected police brutality at the offices of the United Party for National Development. Journalists must be permitted to conduct their work without fear of reprisal.

The Board was concerned to hear that New Vision reporter Elijah Mumba was beaten during an August 2016 assignment, and that media watchdog Misa¬Zambia chairman Hellen Mwale was summoned for questioning after issuing a statement on the assault. The arrest of Kashiki, compounded by the censorious effect of Mwale's summoning, sends a chilling message to Zambian media, which runs contrary to President Lungu's claim that he is a "staunch defender" of media freedom...."

Apprehended and detained at Kabwata Police Station

Covering the committal to the High Court of former Lusaka Province minister Obvious Mwaliteta accused of aggravated robbery with other persons, and another case involving UPND vice-president Geoffrey Bwalya Mwamba at the Lusaka Magistrates' Court Complex on August 26, 2016, a MUVI Television crew and I were apprehended and detained at Kabwata Police Station for about two hours.

GBM, as he is popularly known, was appearing at court after he was quoted in the media as having said that he would go for 'President Edgar Lungu's throat'. I had been assigned to cover his scheduled appearance at court.

Often in Zambia, when a popular opposition leader is appearing at court, a horde of cadres throng the court premises to offer solidarity. However, also often is the confusion that ensues as a result of these cadres' presence. Police are usually deployed to the courts to maintain peace and order. And on this particular day, there were literally hundreds of police officers keeping vigil at the Lusaka Magistrates' Court Complex.

Pictures of a cohort of police and military officers add a different flavour to a newspaper's design. So, as this clique of police officers converged and received a briefing on how to go about their duties at the court, I took pictures. At the same time, my colleagues from MUVI TV also filmed the officers.

So, after I had already taken a few shots of the event, one senior officer took notice of my presence. He asked me to give him my camera but I opted not to respond. And before he could say another word, his lieutenants had already pounced on me. They hit me on the wrist and chest with the butt of a gun, forcing me to let go of the camera which they later confiscated. Simultaneously, other officers bundled MUVI TV's Naomi Ng'andu-Mweemba and Mwaka Ndawa into a police van and confiscated their camera.

As I attempted to reason with the senior officer, trying to explain that I was simply doing my work, two of his over-excited subordinates hit me again with the gun, demanding that I stop "troubling" their *bwana* (boss). The senior officer later handed me the camera and asked me to delete all pictures I had taken of his officers. I did just that and showed him I had deleted them. He then ordered his subordinates to bundle me into the same van as my MUVI TV colleagues.

When I was being dragged to the van, I secretly removed the memory card from the camera and handed it to my workmate Abigail Sitenge. The officers were unaware that she was a journalist and neither did they see me hand her the memory card as it was done in the twinkling of an eye.

We were driven to Kabwata Police Station where we were quizzed on what we intended to do with the pictures and footage of the police officers. We explained that for us, police presence at court always made news. We 'apologised' for filming the officers. They again demanded that the footage and pictures be deleted. However, Naomi's camera had a low battery and suddenly went off. She could not delete the footage on the camera unless there was access to a computer. Incredibly, the entire Kabwata Police Station, in the heart of the capital city Lusaka, did not have a computer. And so this became another issue.

They turned to me and asked me to delete my pictures. And that was it.

They, thus, remained with the unresolved issue of the MUVI TV crew and its camera with a flat battery. After having seemingly satisfied them with my 'remorse' for taking pictures, the three of us were released after about two hours. The MUVI TV reporters were taken to their station by police officers who made sure that footage of their presence at court was deleted.

Thanks to technology, I was able to restore my camera images with a picture restoring software. I shared them with the MUVI TV reporters who intelligently compiled and ran them in their report. *The Post* too, published them.

For how long will M'membe 'insult' the President?

This may seem funny, yet it's true. Suspected PF supporters once got away with my only K100.

My third encounter with the wrath of youths clad in PF regalia—or

CHAPTER ONE

'defenders of the President' as they called themselves—was at the Lusaka Civic Centre in 2016 during the installation ceremony of councillors, council chairpersons, the deputy mayor and Mayor Wilson Kalumba.

In the company of my then workmate and former school classmate Patrick Chilambwe-Mulenga, I arrived at the Civic Centre where the ceremony was scheduled to take place. I immediately set about doing my work, taking pictures of the officials who were being installed. Among them was President Edgar Lungu's daughter, Tasila, Chawama's Nkoloma ward councillor.

As I looked round the venue to see who else had attended the function, a gentleman approached me and asked me to follow him. Sensing something was amiss; I bluntly declined and decided to move to the centre where the main activities were taking place. But this guy was bold; he followed me to the centre where I pretended to be busy taking pictures. He later retreated after failing to rough me up in front of home affairs minister Stephen Kampyongo, police officers and other personalities that had gathered to witness the ceremony.

Why didn't I report this intimidating character? Well, knowing how 'powerful' some cadres were, I suspected nothing would have been done by the police. It did not seem necessary.

A 'renowned' PF cadre, Stanley Chumya, soon approached me and asked me to follow him. At this point, I sensed that I was not wanted at that event. I sensed that someone knew I was from *The Post* and they feared I would report that which they may not have wanted reported. Then after a while trying to figure out how to leave the place, I saw Lusaka Province Youth Chairman, Kennedy Kamba. I saw him seated in the tent as he looked around and watched overzealous youths fail to make me leave that place.

I gathered courage and went to Kamba, walking past Kampyongo who smiled at me. I told Kamba that his people were planning to attack me. His response confirmed my fears. "For how long will you be used by M'membe?" he asked on top of his voice. "He is just using you to fight his enemies. For how long will M'membe insult President? Just stop working for M'membe; he won't manage fighting the President for the next five years. And what will you benefit?" His loud tone drew attention. He advised that I leave immediately, warning that if I didn't, I would be responsible for whatever the youths would do to me as there was only little he could do to help me out.

With everyone's attention on us, I walked away from the tent, with shame and fear inscribed on my face. But I was afraid of leaving the Civic Centre. The cadres had already gathered and were waiting for me to leave so that they could sort me out. Then one muscular man dressed in a grey suit walked to where I was and offered to see me off to a place where I could be picked up by the company vehicle. As this was going on, Patrick Chilambwe-Mulenga was in hiding. I had thought he would come to my aid but he was scared of being hounded, so, he watched from the crowd.

As I was walked to where the driver would pick me up from, the cadres started following us. It turned out that the guy who was seeing me off was, in fact, their leader—'boss', they called him. They started pushing me around but he ordered them to stop, telling them that the minister had instructed him to allow me to leave unhurt. The cadres were not happy and some punched me in the ribs.

Noticing I was in trouble, renowned freelance photographer Jean-Serg Mandela rushed to where I was being harassed and asked for 'his parcels'—my phones and camera. I looked at him and quickly understood what he wanted me to do. He thought the cadres might beat me and get away with my phones and camera. I handed them over to him and all the cadres said to him was, "don't even think of taking pictures of us, we will beat you". Mandela walked away. The cadres' 'boss' gave up on defending me and he too left. I was all alone.

Just when it dawned on me that I was going to be beaten, they asked me for money and said, "If you give us money, we will leave you and no one will touch you." I recalled that I had a K100 note in my pockets and so, I pulled it out and gave it to them. The PF youths began arguing over the money. As they did so, I ran. Mandela reappeared and helped me escape the scene via the Civic Centre workers' car park. My office transport had arrived to pick me and Chilambwe-Mulenga up and we sped off on Independence Avenue.

This was my last duty in active journalism practice. From then on, I decided to take a back seat. However, I have not quit practicing journalism. I feel the skill is in me and believe my contribution to the practice adds some flavour to the profession. I therefore encourage those studying journalism to remain brave and help stir their talents with those already existing in the journalism field. Also, I encourage those studying journalism, and those new in the field of journalism practice, to at all costs, try and avoid covering events that pose a danger on their lives. Like they say, there is no story worth a journalist's life.

This profession, like you may have been taught in school, is not as lucrative as you might have imagined. In this field, you don't run away when there is a fracas; you remain and document it, until you observe the environment is getting unfavourable horrific. You need to be strategic and befriend police officers, nurses, doctors, politicians and street children. This is a profession you may choose (or not choose) based on your conviction.

CHAPTER TWO

Journey from church to Dundumwezi

DUNDUMWEZI came to prominence during the general elections in August 2016. Dundumwezi, a constituency in Kalomo district of Southern Province of Zambia, had a total number of 40,155 registered voters. The constituency shot to fame after UPND presidential candidate Hakainde Hichilema polled a whopping 30,810 of 31,707 total votes cast. The PF candidate, Edgar Lungu secured only a paltry 252 votes, with the remaining votes split among seven other candidates.

The day the Dundumwezi results were announced, the constituency became a household name; somehow expressing how much love the people of that area had for Hichilema.

By this time, The Post Newspapers had been shut down by the Zambia Revenue Authority (ZRA). Staff had, however, continued to gather outside the shuttered premises on Bwinjimfumu Road. Seated in parked cars or on chairs and tables provided by well-wishers, we operated on

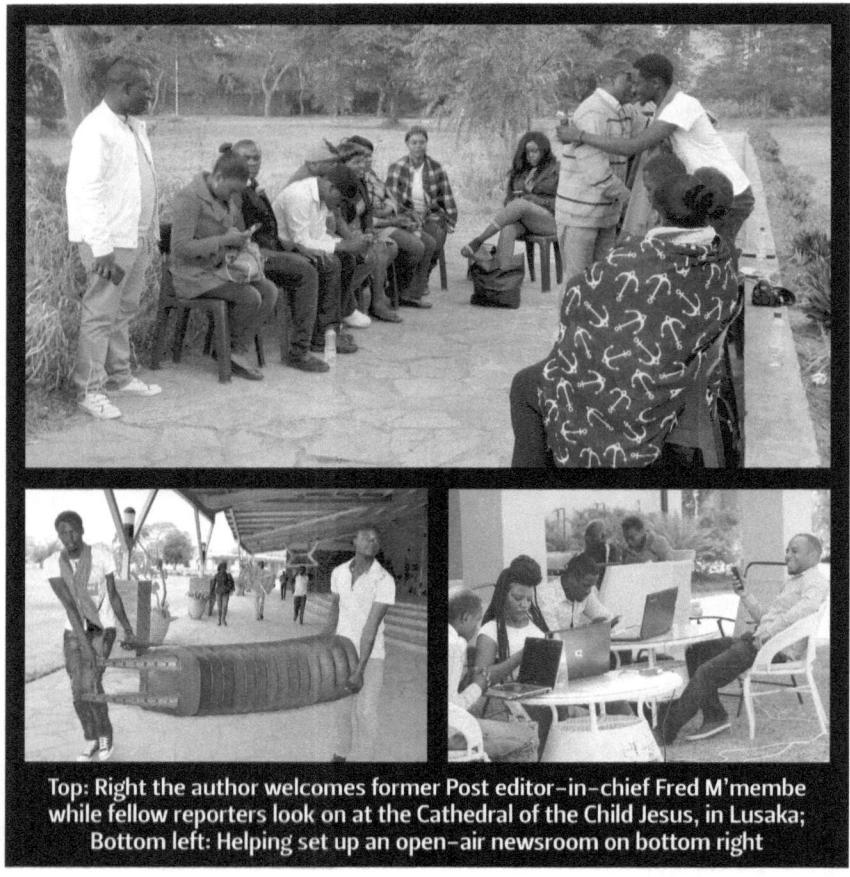

Top: Right the author welcomes former Post editor-in-chief Fred M'membe while fellow reporters look on at the Cathedral of the Child Jesus, in Lusaka; Bottom left: Helping set up an open-air newsroom on bottom right

an 'open-air' newsroom.

Going on about with our usual work of gathering news and writing stories, a Rosa bus with suspected PF cadres drove down a crescent off Bwinjimfumu Road and parked briefly before making a U-turn.

We immediately sensed danger. Our editors contacted Lusaka Province police commissioner Nelson Phiri, seeking protection, but his response was, "we cannot protect you right now. Just move away from there and find where to go." Deprived of this expected police protection, we immediately gathered our tables, chairs and equipment and drove off. In a sense, this marked the beginning of our plight as 'fugitive journalists.'

We were now in the PF's cross hairs and this marked the beginning of a long difficult journey. Our first stop in this journey was the Cathedral of the Child Jesus, a Catholic Church situated about five kilometres from Bwinjimfumu Road.

It is a large sprawling area, with a Church, priests' quarters and several offices. Arriving there, we unpacked the chairs, tables and equipment and set up another 'open-air' newsroom right behind the Church building while our editors consulted management on how best they could help us.

However, because of how political *The Post* closure issue was perceived, the Church was reluctant to allow us to set up a working base there. But, after hours of begging them, we were allowed to stay "just for a few days."

However, after several days in the dusty open space was, and left exposed to the scorching sun, our supervisors started looking for an alternative venue. So, a few days later, an alternative venue was found in Kabulonga and we shifted immediately. We worked from Kabulonga for several few weeks until we finally found another place to rent for as long as we could manage. We nicknamed our secret working place 'Dundumwezi'.

This remained the place we could run to when our safety as Post journalists was at risk. However, soon came the unexpected final nail in *The Post*'s coffin. Five former employees decided to file a petition in the courts of law claiming the company was failing to pay them their salaries and benefits. The judge then appointed the provisional liquidator, and *The Post* was placed under liquidation.

QUIT! A test of comradeship

The closure of The Post on June 21, 2016 marked the beginning of a tough season for those of us who worked there. At some point, it seemed so surreal, like an unending nightmare. I thought the Zambia Revenue Authority (ZRA) would eventually re-open the institution. However, it was not to be. To this day, Zambia's largest selling privately-owned

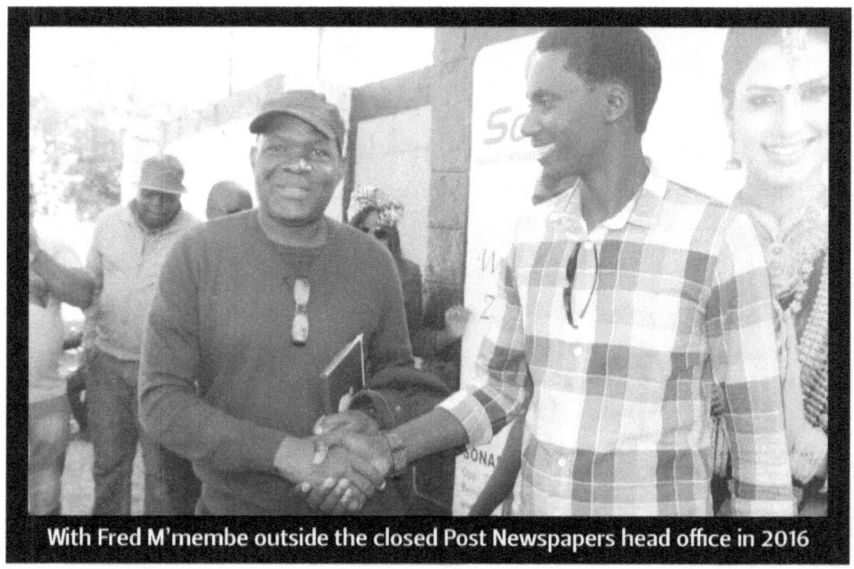
With Fred M'membe outside the closed Post Newspapers head office in 2016

newspaper remains closed. Events that led to that fateful day in June 2016 saw the commencement of comradeship trials.

We confidently assured our 'friends' that cared to ask, regarding the way forward, that the company would be reopened sooner than expected because it was not a *kantemba* (makeshift shop) kind of newspaper that would be shut in the manner it had. Personally, I never thought it would get this far. But as the days grew to weeks and then months, it began to sink in that there may not be a future for *The Post*. The days of *The Post* may have come to an end.

I began to realise something. Many of those that called 'us' either for coverage or merely to check on us when *The Post* was thriving, all disappeared. Government sources, celebrities, even friends from the public and private media, stopped associating with us.

Our six months of operation under the closed Post Newspaper were heartbreaking. Despite all the many negative things people said about him, it was Dr Fred M'membe who was our strength during those trying months. The experience was thrilling; we mingled more and cemented our comradeships further. We worked as though we were brothers and sisters. And for many of us, this seemed like a revolution.

We had our meals outside the closed newspaper's premises and work continued from the 'open-air' newsroom where well-wishers and sympathisers often offered us food or drink to keep us going in weather that varied from extreme cold, windy, to scorching heat.

However, this period also exposed individuals for who they really were. Inevitably, there were those who were ready to betray their colleagues. These were identified and we learnt how to deal with them.

As weeks wore on, many of our previously reliable sources began to decline interviews. They disassociated themselves from us, as though we had become lepers. Many of these were our colleagues in the media. We could not cover assignments freely because some people were making fun of us, saying our newspaper was petty. But I always believed that we were heroic and would make it despite all the negativity.

Some of our friends even advised us to just leave Dr M'membe and let him fight his battles alone. They advised us to just quit and look for jobs elsewhere. They told us, "*Muzafela mbolo ya shamwali*" (you will pay for what you didn't do, just leave The Post). They said we were helping Dr M'membe fight his personal battles and that we had become as malicious as he was. "You're too young to engage 'political heavy-weights' in battles you don't understand," some said. The many things these 'friends' said triggered extensive reflection among many of us that worked for The Post.

But for many of us at the Post, the question deep in our hearts was, "If I leave, where do I go?"

"If we quit writing stories in line with our newspaper policy," I wondered, "what happens? Who pays me and for what?" Ultimately, I realised that their advice was centred on impressing their own paymasters. Many of this advice mainly came from those in the public media and those in government institutions; few from the independent media gave similar counsel.

However, what these people forgot was that a journalist always did their work according to the organisation's editorial policy. It always seemed funny how people suggested that I quit working for The Post, as though they were going to offer me an alternative job.

This is how I lost the many friends I had while The Post was fully functional. They all disappeared because they could not stand with someone who was working for a newspaper perceived to have been fighting 'political heavyweights'. The comradeship test ended just like that; friends could not stand with us and instead walked out on us.

So, these were the things I went through as a reporter for the once critical and vibrant Post newspaper. As journalists, it is always cardinal to uphold media ethics and objectivity in the discharge of our duties. Dedication to duty and courage is something that one must nurture to face the challenges that the Zambian media industry is currently grappling with.

You see, Dr M'membe's entrepreneurial mind gave me an opportunity to work in a competitive environment. *The Post* newspaper environment awoke my diagnostic and critical mind. I was able to put up this project because of the priceless training I underwent as a journalist at the "paper that digs deeper". I shall forever hold the skills I acquired so dear to my heart. While working for *The Post*, several senior reporters and editors helped nurture my then young talent into what I hold onto firmly today; I am grateful to M'membe—as we called him—for this.

CHAPTER THREE

Bare breasts in front of my camera

IT AROUSED debate among social media maniacs owing to its 'hot' scenery. It was all tweeted and re-tweeted, Facebooked and shared. Instagram too was not left out. There simply was pandemonium, both on public buses and private transport and went viral on almost all social media platforms.

With a sparkling smile befitting a toothpaste advert, she appeared on the catwalk. Whistling, applauding and wailing, the audience seemed unease. Seated adjacent to an erected red-carpet stage, young and middle-aged men and women pulled out their smartphones to 'smartly' capture the exciting stature walking past them.

Through my camera lens, I too saw her walk down the red carpet; I silently chuckled, took multiple shots, previewed the images then lowered my camera to see with my bare eyes as the topless finalist flaunted her assets at the 2014 Miss Freedom of the World Beauty Pageant held at the Taj Pamodzi Hotel in Lusaka on March 21.

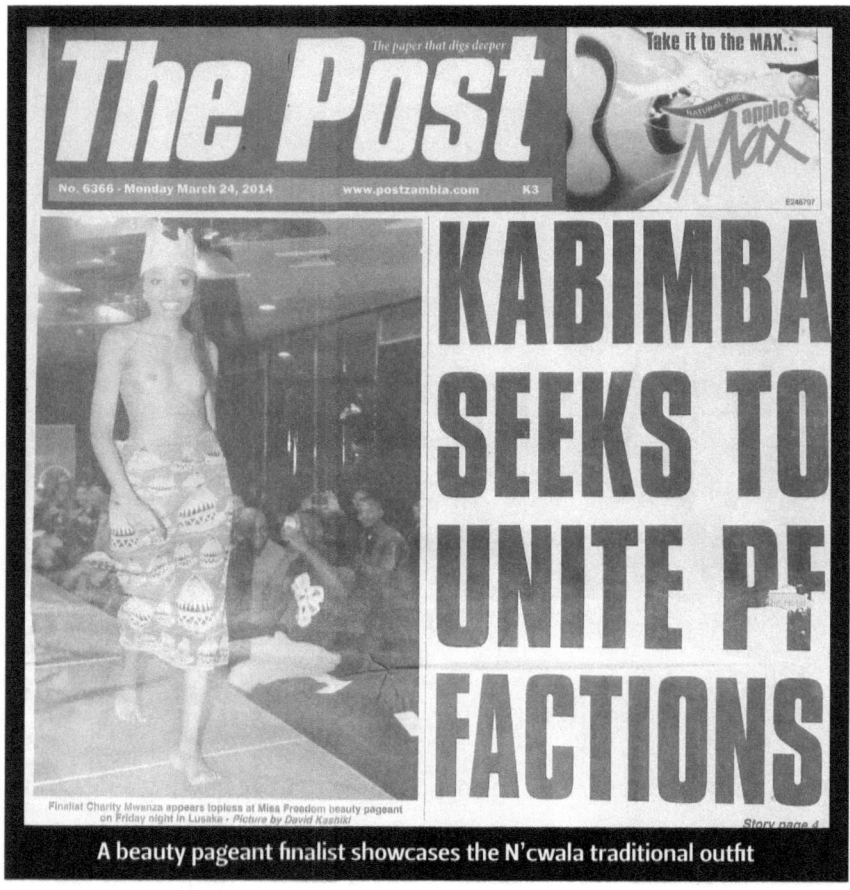

A beauty pageant finalist showcases the N'cwala traditional outfit

Wearing a reddish-brown chitenge material from her waist down, Charity Mwanza came down the catwalk. She was bare-breasted, bare-foot and had a Ngoni head dress partially covering her black breads. Her appearance reminded me of the bare-breasted Ngoni women at the annual N'cwala ceremony, but her firm breasts were the distinction.

As she strode down the red carpet with the confidence of a diva, snapping her fingers in time with a steady R'n'B beat, I positioned myself to take several photos. In spite of the adrenalin running, I managed to capture the picture. With confidence, she walked, spun round to show all gathered what she had in store. For those that attended the pageant, Charity's appearance probably stole the show.

CHAPTER THREE

As a photojournalist covering that event, it was not an easy assignment. It was a difficult one as it involved ethical judgment on nudity. But I saved that controversy for later.

The following morning, I was at the office. I broke the news about what had happened the previous evening. I told my workmates about a contestant who had walked bare-breasted down the catwalk, and that I had taken pictures of the incident.

My colleagues, both male and female, jostled to my workspace to catch a glimpse of the images. "These are brilliant pictures for the front page," they said. "Submit them for publication". And I did just that.

Because it was a weekend, the picture was reserved for Monday's edition when more people would want to buy the paper. And that Monday, the picture ran on the front page. Reaction was swift, sharp and varied.

Numerous people got to know of me after that picture was published. Then, women organisations that wanted to find out what my intention was for taking that picture started calling the office, wanting to speak to me.

Alice Rowland-Musukwa, the organiser of the pageant, also came under fire for allowing Charity to participate semi-nude. "People should not condemn Charity Mwanza without trying to understand the context in which she bared her chest," Rowland-Musukwa said. "It was not in public but in an event where models showcased various Zambian traditional wear. Whereas many people accept the baring of chests during N'cwala, they should not forget that Charity chose to showcase the N'cwala outfit during the Miss Freedom pageant; she was in a role-play. And as organisers, we spoke to her about it before she appeared topless, she was aware we invited photographers and she told us she was comfortable with it. Her family was there too. So, the public should look at this from a positive perspective."

Provoked by her picture, friends and unknown people contacted me to ask for Charity's number. Her bare breasts had earned her indisputable fame and notoriety. Despite having her number, I never gave it out nor contacted her. I strove hard to remain professional and protect a young lady whose intentions were to showcase a traditional outfit and not expose her to 'vultures'.

Despite drawing all the attention at that event, Charity did not win. At the time of authoring this book, she was a fashion designer and founder of Charine Designs.

This author, however, later contacted Charity Mwanza for an interview on her experience at the March 21, 2014 event and she had this to say:

"It was not easy for me to contend life after I appeared on the front page of *The Post* newspaper; because many people misinterpreted it. But I can confess to you that the only people who were there for me, when that picture of me walking topless on stage was published, were my mother, my sisters and part of my friends. My father was very upset with me. He was like Charity, please; your actions are being discussed on the radio, TV and newspapers. Look what you've put our family name in. The words that followed my walking topless injured my family so much. Some people called me a prostitute; others said I would not get married and just many people said all sorts of nasty things about me. I can tell you that some friends left me and some demonised me. However, there were some people that comforted me; they consoled me when I was being described in hurtful terms."

When asked if she ever regretted walking topless, Charity Mwanza swiftly said, "I do not regret going topless and I will never regret it."

"You know, before I bared my chest at that event, I had been looking forward to being featured on ZNBC's Smooth Talk to just talk about fashion and modelling. But I didn't have a way to get there for an interview. Now, when I walked topless at that pageant contest, Innocent Kalaluka himself came looking for me and not me looking for him for an interview as the situation was earlier. I had been itching to being interviewed on Smooth Talk. And you know, when that happened, some people said that it was my ladder to my lows, but hey, I thank God that when that happened, did happen to my advantage. It helped me up the ladder and today, I have a wide clientele base all coming to Charine Designs for their wedding, kitchen party and other designer outfits. It worked for me to go higher," she added.

When asked on how her father came to terms with her 'nudes' in the papers and social media, Charity said, "After he met his friends at some place, apparently they discussed me and he was made to understand that my intention was not to corrupt morals but to showcase a Ngoni woman's traditional outfit. So, he came home and told me that I needed to hold my head high and that all was going to be well with time. He advised me not to listen to any negative words people would tell me; he told me, maintain your focus and passion. And from that moment on, he gave me courage because for about three days, we had not been talking."

"Let me tell you this; when *The Post* published a picture of the topless and firm-breasted me; only God knows the number of men that called to ask me out, some of them ministers you would be shocked if I mentioned their names here. But I wasn't for sale, I didn't appear to portray I was a sex object. I think that is where we are lagging in Zambia; we think when that happens then a lady is a slut, no. Can you imagine; they all wanted to date me and where they got my number, to date I don't know! But ultimately, I concluded that even if people are scolding me today, I'm sure they were happy to see me that way although most of them pretended not to have been happy to see my firm breasts," Charity Mwanza shared and laughed.

"I have changed a lot and I'm happy that very soon, I will be getting married and most of all, I'm happy that my fiancé accepts me despite all of my past flaws." The 24-year-old fashion designer remarked.

Dancing with the President: music and politics in Zambia

Barrack Obama used Stevie Wonder's 'Signed, Sealed, Delivered I'm Yours' during his successful 2008 presidential campaign.

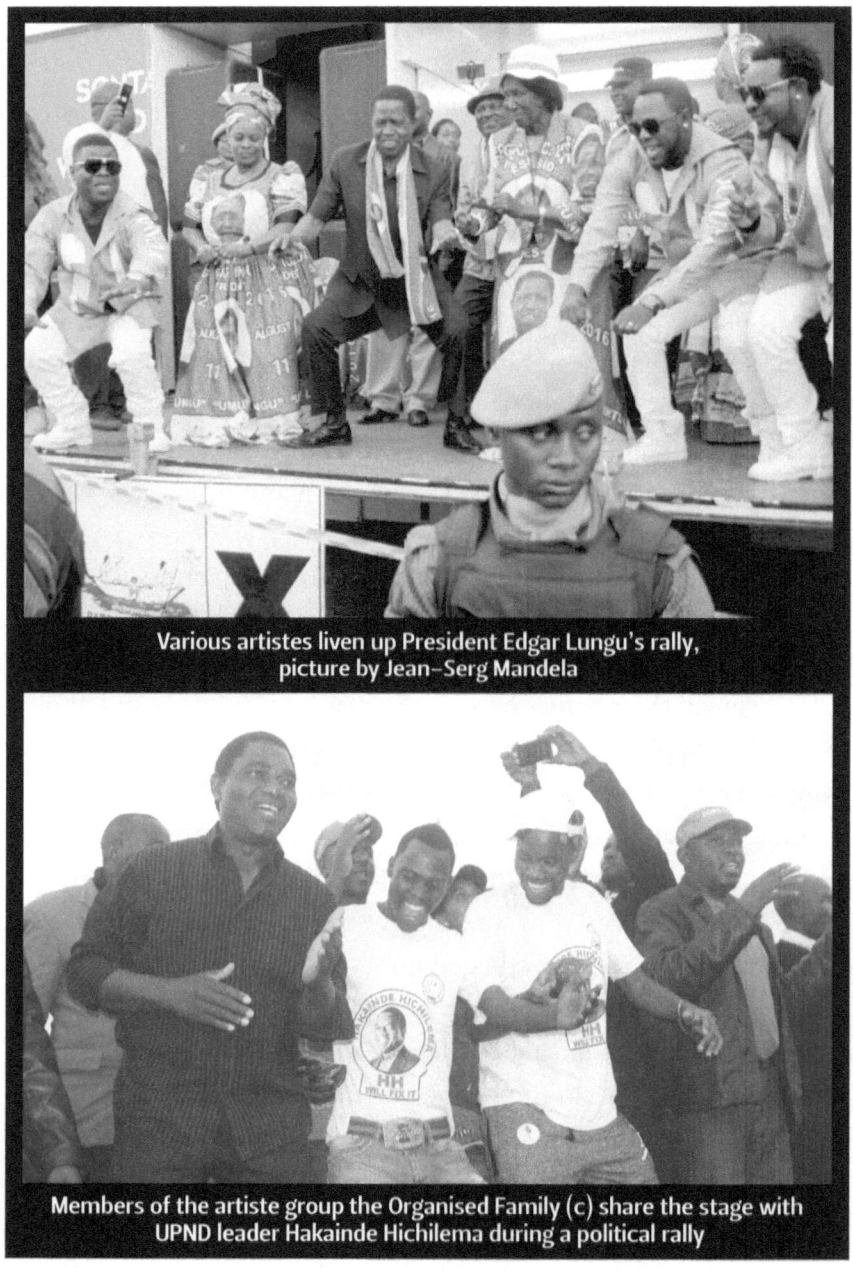

Various artistes liven up President Edgar Lungu's rally, picture by Jean–Serg Mandela

Members of the artiste group the Organised Family (c) share the stage with UPND leader Hakainde Hichilema during a political rally

First Republican president Dr Kenneth Kaunda and other freedom fighters in Zambia, used Tiyende Pamodzi, a Nyanja song calling for unity before and after independence. Then in the early 1990s, the late

CHAPTER THREE

Frederick Chiluba and the MMD (then in opposition) used PK Chishala's *Common Man*, as the song to help them communicate the social injustices that characterised the Kaunda regime.

In 2011, PF founder and former Republican President Michael Sata used Dandy Krazy's *Don't Kubeba*. Sata's successor, President Edgar Lungu used *Dununa Reverse,* a song by JK and others during his campaigns in 2016.

All these are some of the clearest instances that have proved that music possesses unique power to inspire, motivate and energise a campaign—whether it's political or social activism. It is also important to mention that these instances cited here are not the first to have successfully used music during campaigns; this trend dates as back as the 1800s.

Music undeniably influences political and ritual movements. As you may be aware, political music expresses anti-government sentiments or protest arguments or represents pro-establishment messages. And from time immemorial, music has either been tolerated by the establishment or simply banned.

Columnist, Jack Mwewa in his article published in the *Times of Zambia* on January 16, 2016, highlighted some of the songs that were banned from radio play and observed that not all songs banned were political, but that, that some songs were banned for fear of them polluting morals.

"Much as we can talk about the then music banned for its contents, a lot of songs playing on radio today could be banned for obscenity and generally inferior quality. Times of Zambia staffer, Austin Kaluba, while domiciled in the United Kingdom once highlighted some songs banned from Zambia Broadcasting Services, the forerunner of Zambia National Broadcasting Corporation radio, which included 'Shebeen King' by Rikki Ililonga. The Censorship Board felt the song was too vulgar with its opening lines: I went to the market/after sunset/ I met Anna/ A girl from Ghana/ I said wha' do you wanna/ She said she wanted a banana." No one was fooled by the banana Rikki was singing about. *'Olemekedzeka'* by the same musician was a hard-hit-

ting political song lampooning corrupt politicians who promised the electorate heaven, but when voted into power ended up abusing their powers and stealing money. 'Nkaizutule' by Lusaka Radio Band was also banned for being vulgar. So was 'Finshi Wingachita' by the late Emmanuel Mulemena.

"The song asks in ci-Bemba –finshi wingachita ngawasanga umunobe bali nabakashi balesamba amenshi ayakaba (what would you do if you found your wife having a hot bath with your friend? Again, the Censorship Board was not fooled by the 'hot bath' Mulemena was talking about. A political hit 'Imisango yaba Chaimani' by the late Max Mwansa, about a ward chairperson who was a wizard, thief and loafer was banned when United National Independence Party (UNIP) leaders complained of its anti-UNIP lyrics. The ban of 'Imisango yaba Chaimani' was later lifted by President Kenneth Kaunda himself who even sang some lines publicly."

In Africa, artistes and private citizens' rights to express their opinions are often violated. This is despite these rights in the case of Zambia, being backed by the Bill of Human Rights (1996), under Article 20 (1) of the Constitution which states in part, "*except with his own consent, no person shall be hindered in the enjoyment of his freedom of expression, that is to say, freedom to hold opinions without interference, freedom to receive ideas and information without interference, freedom to impart and communicate to the public generally or to any person or class of persons, and freedom from interference with his correspondence.*"

There are many instances where musicians have expressed their opinions in songs. Some have had their works banned from radio or the musicians themselves have been arrested for merely expressing their opinions through music. Such violations of rights are not only exerted on artistes but even on private citizens who also attempt to express their rights.

For example, *Anyandule*, a song from Petersen Zagaze's 2007 album *Bobojani*, brought about talk resulting in public radio not playing the song because of the its political connotations. The IMPI too, had many

CHAPTER THREE

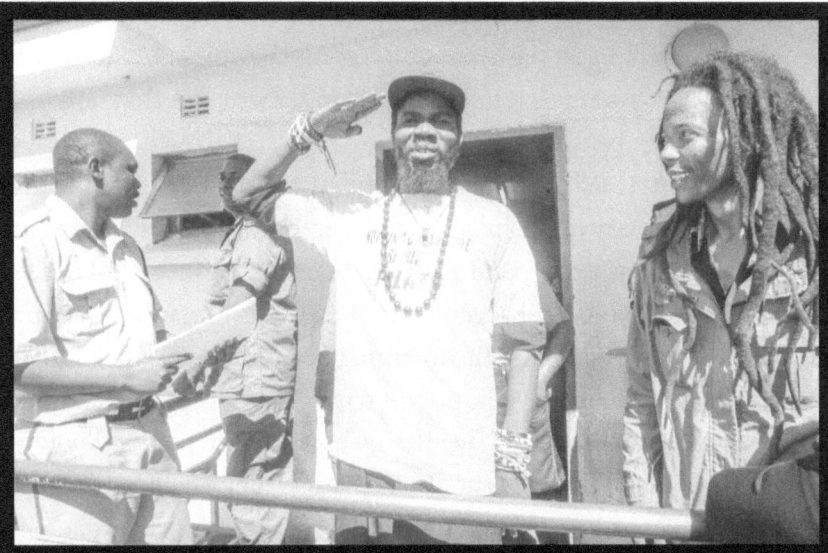

Chama Fumba (Pilato) gestures his fans shortly after being granted bail in his conduct likely to breach the peace case. On his left are police officers and right, is former Zambia Association of Musicians Maiko Zulu

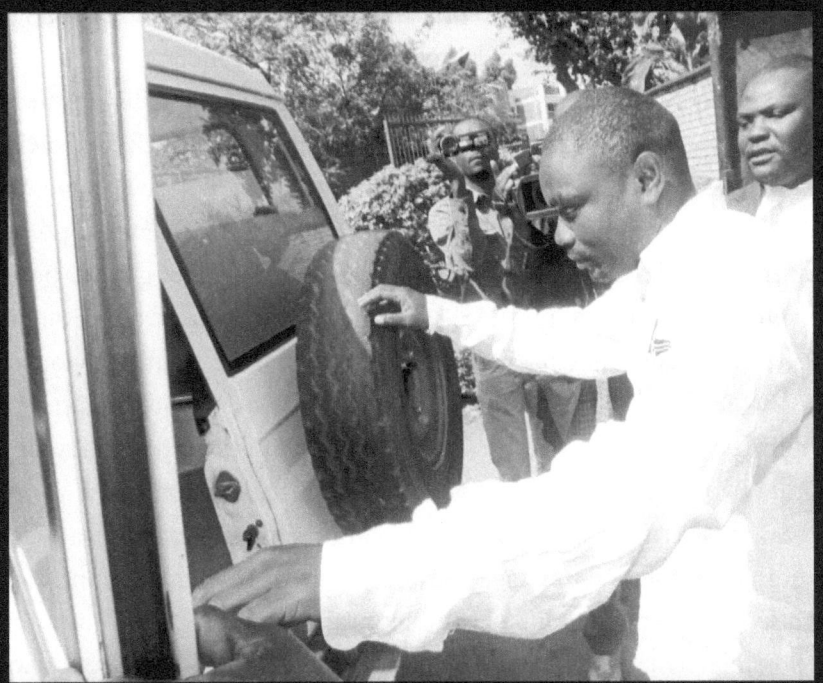

Clifford Dimba (General Kanene) goes back to jail after appearing in his defilement appeal case at the Lusaka High Court

of its songs not playing on public and some private radio stations on similar reasons a Petersen's songs. Among the songs by IMPI is *Ba Sakala Nyongo*, a song that talks about lying politicians that only visit electorates when begging for votes.

When Pilato (real name Chama Fumba) released his song *Alungu anabwera*, a parody of Nashil Pichen Kazembe's 1970s hit, he was arrested and charged with 'conduct likely to cause the breach of peace', a charge he was later discharged of by the Lusaka Magistrate's Court. The lyrics of the song depict the dilemma of a politician called Lungu, who came from Chawama compound with a suitcase full of a popular whisky brand, Jameson, and eventually ascended to power following the death of a leader, but this politician had no idea on how to govern.

Other artistes like Clifford Dimba, commonly known as 'General Kanene', reacted to Alungu anabwera, a song that criticised President Lungu and his government by releasing a song titled, *Ulemu* (respect). But Kanene's response was to praise the Head of State and his government and highlighted the need to respect the Presidency.

At the time, Kanene was in prison serving an 18-year jail term for defiling a 14-year-old schoolgirl. However, in July 2015, while on a visit to Mukobeko Maximum Security Prison in Kabwe where Kanene was incarcerated, President Lungu pardoned the singer and later appointed him an ambassador—ironically—in the fight against gender based violence, an appointment the Head of State later revoked after Kanene faced a court case alleging he had committed violence against a woman.

The timing of the pardon raised many eyebrows. And at that time, the public speculated as to the reasons President Lungu pardoned Kanene, who was only one year into his sentence for defiling a minor.

So, music in an election year or campaign season summarises a candidate's political messages or policies in an entertaining and captivating manner. This kind of campaign labours to woo as many voters as possible, hence political party campaign managers sometimes broker deals with artistes that have a wide following.

They do so to ensure that undecided voter that may not like their candidate, would vote for the party on the premise that their favourite artiste shared the stage with that candidate. This also applies to other notable personalities such as sports stars that attend campaign rallies with a view to helping boost chances for the preferred candidate.

This practice of engaging artistes on the campaign trail is pursued both by the ruling and opposition parties.

Because of this, some artistes in Zambia have lost their following because of 'aligning' themselves with political parties during campaigns. And for those artistes that dance right and with the 'correct' politicians, they often emerge from the campaigns richer and more powerful than before.

The onus is ultimately on the individual artiste to choose who they want to dine with but not forget the ordinary fan who is drawn more to their idol's art than their political views.

CHAPTER FOUR

Reportage and objectivity in Zambian media

"*NEWSPAPERS, in particular, have a long-standing practice of endorsing candidates in competitive political races. Although some readers think these endorsements signal bias in the publication's news coverage, Society of Professional Journalists encourages editorial pages to promote thoughtful debate on candidates and politics; letting readers know the newspaper's vision is part of that discussion.*

"Reporters are not columnists or editorial writers. SPJ's recommendation is that reporters not take a position on an issue, or in a candidate's race that they are covering. They may do so privately, but they definitely should not do so in a public or visible way," reads part of an article published on www.spj.org that sought to discuss media ethics.

These are the words of Society of Professional Journalists vice-chairman Fred Brown, who has covered national and international politics for over 40 years and wrote the above for the SPJ ethics committee.

When you first get to journalism school, you will be asked questions like "What is objectivity? What are ethics?" You will even be asked to define the word "objective", among other journalism building components.

According to the Oxford English Living Dictionaries, "objective" is defined as (of a person or their judgment) not influenced by personal feelings or opinions in considering and representing facts. Objectivity is the quality of simply being objective.

The dictionary further defines Ethics as, "a moral principle that governs a person's behaviour or the conducting of an activity."

Having defined these key terms, let's discuss them with particular bias to the Zambian media fraternity and partially, in the international media circles.

In discussing whether it is ethical for a newspaper to directly or indirectly endorse a candidate in an election, we need to highlight an objective perspective to the issue at hand with the help of a philosophical statement; the means justify the ends and or vice versa.

The media at large play a pivotal role in the improvement or degeneration of society. Therefore, the media acts as a platform for easy access to and dissemination of credible information. Among the media's key roles include educating and informing the public. In this respect, during an election year, this platform must be utilised responsibly to equip the ordinary person with the relevant credible information to enable them to make an informed decision regarding their potential president, parliamentarian, mayor, civic leaders and so forth.

With this at hand, there is need for the media, if it is to be objective, to, in the run-up to an election, write and publish profiles of candidates in that year's election. For example, in Zambia newspapers and television stations can publish or broadcast profiles of candidates like key political candidates, among others, for the purpose of educating the masses on the politician's beliefs, ideals, their failures and successes in both their private and professional lives.

And from this, a media house may select and endorse a candidate and promote them to the ordinary citizen. If a decision is made for the greater good of the nation, there is no harm; the end has literally justified the means. If one is objective enough, they would deduce that there is nothing wrong with a media house endorsing a political party's presidential candidate, provided there is something that justifies the end. If people are furnished with the above information, even if a politician moves in to clamp down on private media, the people would rise to their defence.

Mr Brown's advice to the SPJ ethics committee adds to the many scholars that have no objections with newspapers' endorsements of political candidates. However, if Zambian media is to take this internationally recognised practice, it has to be seen to be objective and impartial.

Zambians need to be educated objectively, truthfully and intensively if they are to make informed decisions. The Zambian people are starved of information. They have no truth heading their side. The only truth and information they are aware of is often what the media owners have decided for them, which is usually the information they feel the people must listen to or read about. The other kind of information the ordinary people receive is that which the government has decided they should know and not what they need to know. For objective and truthful media pundits, the media is the answer to all that is happening to people in today's society.

Today, if you asked media practitioners, both from the private or public sector, whether objectivity, ethics or truthfulness exist in their media house, they would have difficulties giving a clear and objective response.

In simple and blunt terms, the Zambian media fraternity in the 21st Century, does not know objectivity, truthfulness or impartiality. Reportage is based on what benefits them and that which does not is demonised.

I can confidently state here that objectivity in Zambian media has never existed in its entirety. The percentage of its existence is too minimal to be noticed. It would purely be illusional or comedic if one alleged that it at one instance existed. Let me prove this point to you with the most recent situations below.

In his book A Robust Think Tank for Africa, Francis Chishala, a Zambian Catholic Jesuit, observed that corruption is only corruption when you are not benefiting from it. The media in this country and its coverage of corruption is selective; media owners won't report on corruption that benefits their businesses. Meanwhile, the corruption they end up reporting on is that which their competitors are benefiting from.

With this attitude in the fourth estate, the fight against corruption may remain futile for as long as we—the media as conduits of information—do not stand for the whole truth. Impartiality demands that if one can't be objective when faced with situations that demand factual reporting, declaring interest and letting others handle the matter truthfully and objectively is the best thing to do. Corruption must be condemned and fought regardless of its perpetrators.

This topic, anyhow, cannot be talked about in its entirety without mentioning some of the key players in Zambia's media industry. These include journalist/accountant/lawyer Dr Fred M'membe, former proprietor and editor-in-chief of the liquidated Post newspapers; veteran journalist Richard Sakala, the former press aide of late president Frederick

Chiluba, and now proprietor of the *Daily Nation* newspaper, and Mr Gerald Shawa, proprietor of Joy FM and Prime Television who gave an interview. The public media too will be included in this dialogue.

Without doubt, the public media—also referred to as the state-owned media—has, during many elections, failed the people of Zambia and this is because of alarming levels of interference by external forces. Issues surrounding the abuses of the public media are in the public domain. Everyone today sees how the public media is abused and how its reporters are more inclined to writing about the ruling party than on reporting stories of public interest.

This situation has the likelihood of continuing until it is deliberately and consciously brought to an end. For as long as powers to appoint the boards that control public media institutions remain with the party in government, such abuses have the potential of being inherited and continued by the United Party for National Development (UPND), Forum of Democracy and Development (FDD), United Progressive Party (UPP), Peoples Party (PP), National Restoration Party (NAREP), Rainbow Party, Party of National Unity (PNU) and other governments in waiting.

Until then, the public media may be excused because it will almost always, stagger to practice objectivity or impartiality for as long as those in government control its content, determine who should be covered and want to tell the public or what they feel the people should know. It is a tool that benefit, mostly those in power as well than those in opposition.

We shall test the objectivity ethos with a brief look at some examples from the 2011 general elections.

In the run-up to those elections, the media in Zambia took a stance and made it clear to everyone whom it perceived was the people's preferred candidate.

Such decisions were inevitably made in line with the particular media house's interests; they wanted to show that their decision to back candidate A was in the people's interest when in reality it was and will always be in their own interest.

The media attached themselves to parties they thought would produce the next President of the Republic of Zambia; a President they felt would be there to promote and protect their business interests and nothing more. The public media, predictably, endorsed the then President Rupiah Banda as the best candidate for the 2011 election.

It has been widely debated whether it is ethically correct for a media house to openly endorse a political party's presidential candidate in a campaign build-up to an election. However, no clear appreciation of the situation has been given to the masses, until today.

Leon Trotsky said, "The end may justify the means as long as there is something that justifies the end." This, using the Zambian media and political arena, is interpreted as meaning that if a media house endorses a candidate in an election, the result must justify the action taken by that media house. There must be general benefits for a country's citizenry; the action must prioritise the interests of the many, as well as the media house's own business interests.

Therefore, there is nothing wrong with a media house endorsing a political party, provided this is done in national interest and decided upon to serve the greater good of the citizenry.

My question to you dear reader is, with regards the decisions made by the various media houses during the 2011 general elections, did the ends justify the means? The answer to this is somewhat a 'small' yes and a 'big' NO! A small yes because their intention was okay when they started it but lost it in the way. And a big NO because when people complained about the government they hoped would change their lives, many media houses gave them no platform; such people received a media blackout. Objectivity in today's heated political environment may be impossible or difficult to attain, but truthfulness should still be a reporter's and media house's ultimate goal.

Zambia, like many African countries, is a young democracy in the hands of a few individuals controlling the affairs of the majority. This country also is not short of those who want to control literally everything. They want to be indirect Heads of State; they want to control the presidency.

M'membe *ayamba* Chagwa, Post *Yagwa* (The Inside View)

'M'membe *ayamba* Chagwa, Post *Yagwa*', (M'membe picks a fight with President Edgar Chagwa Lungu, [and] brings down *The Post*), is a sub-heading aimed at ensuring that you the reader does not miss out any truth or objective piece of information regarding the 'fall' of *The Post*.

Fred M'membe, a critical thinker, and an excellent strategist, may be said to have mismanaged his empire. He and many others have

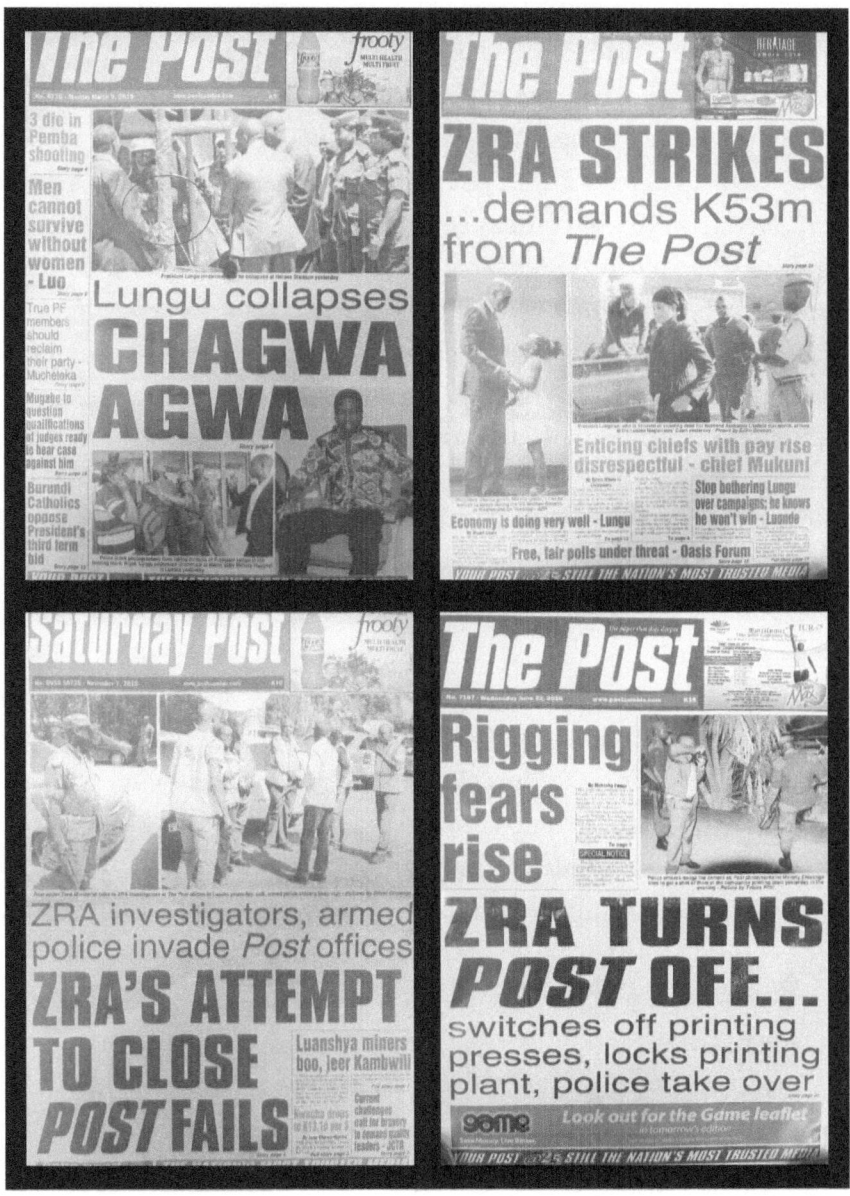

apportioned blame of the predicament The Post found itself in, on government alone, but he and his chain of managers, too, is to blame for the newspaper's 'demise'.

Now, it is cardinal to note here that M'membe being with a strong personality, is a perfect example of people in the world that attempt to control the presidency. He is a 'puppeteer' and an accomplished indoctrinator, or if you like, charmer. It is not a secret that M'membe favours socialist ideologies. As with most socialists, M'membe makes sure his own interests are served first. For so many years, he has been perceived to have used other people to achieve his personal goals. In his book *The Politically Incorrect Guide to Socialism*, Kevin D. Williamson says, *"Socialist central planning always works best for the class that produces the central planners, who can see to it that their own interests are relatively well served...."*

And In his maiden speech to the United Nations General Assembly, commenting on socialism in Venezuela and that country's recent economic situation and peoples suffering, United States President Donald Trump said, *"...The problem in Venezuela is not that socialism has been poorly implemented, but that socialism has been faithfully implemented.*

"From the Soviet Union to Cuba to Venezuela, wherever true socialism or communism has been adopted, it has delivered anguish and devastation and failure. Those who preach the tenets of these discredited ideologies only contribute to the continued suffering of the people who live under these cruel systems."

If you care to examine him well, you may deduce that M'membe and his once close friend Wynter Kabimba fit the description of true socialists. They both proclaim to believe in and espouse socialist values and ideologies.

To many, M'membe is a brilliant journalist one who has fought battles for press freedom with various governments, winning several times and losing a few. That is an outsider's view or perspective of M'membe. For many people like myself that worked for him under *The Post*, he was (is) a brilliant politician behind the newspaper, an accomplished strategist, a celebrated journalist and media entrepreneur. To others however, M'membe was a self-centred editor-in-chief who wanted all things to go his way and ultimately lost grip of his journalistic public sympathy after he exhibited more characteristics of a political opponent than a journalist in Edgar Lungu's face, who at this time had shown interest to collect debt from tax-defaulting companies. This interest was announced at a political rally in Mandevu township.

To bag some respect as a Post journalist, one needed to be an excellent reporter or worker. And in the absence of that, one needed to be on Fred M'membe's good side. His style of leadership at the once 'great' newspaper was centred on what I may loosely describe as "divide and rule".

Those that were relatively sharp, and with excellent boot-licking, rumour-mongering and back-biting talents, made it as star reporters and subsequently as managers. Those that were simply brilliant journalists or workers, were often sidelined from the operations of the institution by his line of managers who, too, adopted his methods of rule, that were seen to be more of a divide-and-rule kind of leadership. And because of this, aspiring managers, editors and others had to adopt his style of leadership if they were to emerge 'powerful' at the company.

At *The Post*, the stories that were most heard in corners were about how some people were remunerated. Most people that got paid handsomely at the institution were those that were close to the 'powers'; at *The Post* favouritism if not nepotism was at its startling levels. This was not an unusual occurrence at the paper as many journalists, among other employees, got accustomed to the leadership style as 'certified' by the editor-in-chief. Some who got 'fat' salaries at *The Post* got them not because they were hard working, but because of their boot-licking tendencies that pleased the establishment. Very few of Post managers rose to their positions based on hard work; most of them were promoted based on their affiliation with those that wielded most authority.

To many former employees that have analysed reasons resulting into the 'hibernation' if not death of the company, The Post Newpapers Limited had ineffectual managers who lacked skills and the backbone to advise M'membe, the major overseer of the institution, on good business practices, including well-timed remittance of taxes to the authorities.

There are some who argue that since *The Post* was his business, he would determine who and how much he paid, regardless of one's contribution to the success and growth of his 'empire'. It was his prerogative, they may claim.

Another fact is that some journalists you may have known as 'stars' through *The Post* may not have been as exceptionally sharp as it may have been portrayed by the institution and other individuals. Because of the need to promote the image of certain individuals, some 'favourite' journalists' bylines were placed on stories they may not even have been aware of. This trend at the newspaper sometimes put innocent reporters in difficult situations, at times resulting in arrests, and harassments just because their byline was on a controversial story. But, it's indisputable, M'membe's newspaper produced some of the best journalists in the country, and his journalistic skill flows in many scribes that worked for him.

It's also important to note that an editor has a right to place his/her reporter's byline on stories they deem fit, when need be.

As earlier stated, among the people that occasioned the liquidation of *The Post* were two senior reporters—Abel Mboozi and Roy Habaalu. Not that this opinion supports the route to have the company liquidated as undertaken by the former workers, but the duo were among the many journalists that were sidelined by the editor-in-chief's stream of editors. M'membe and his line of editors may be said to have seemed to have been deriving pleasure from perturbing journalists that had views independent from theirs.

But that's not to say that the two reporters were among *The Post* journalists that may have had independent views at all, perhaps. Their being sidelined did not result from their 'independent' thinking but simply from a total dislike by those that helped managed if not mismanage the company at the time.

So Habaalu's and Mboozi's 'treachery' came into being after the two were humiliatingly sidelined. When the company was shut by the Zambia Revenue Authority on June 21, 2016, Roy and Abel were among the scribes forcibly put on leave until the company felt it needed their

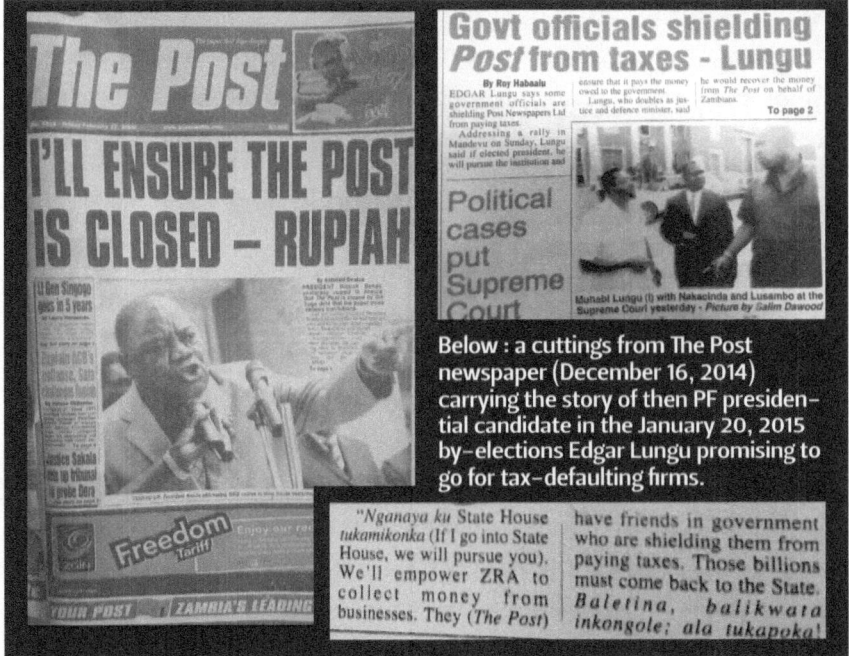

Below : a cuttings from The Post newspaper (December 16, 2014) carrying the story of then PF presidential candidate in the January 20, 2015 by-elections Edgar Lungu promising to go for tax-defaulting firms.

services. Others were called back, but the two, remained in limbo guessing what their fate was to be. To the duo who viewed themselves as senior reporters, this was embarrassing and it somehow signalled dismissal. The reporters that were left to work for the closed newspaper were mostly those that joined the media 'recently' but put up almost the same efforts in news collection as the 'old legs'. I was privileged to have been part of the team that was selected to continue serving the 'seized' company.

However, the decision to have some reporters on leave was meant to protect information of where the company printed the then 'illegal' Post newspapers and where it stored this newspaper among others. This was at a time when the company was in Intensive Care Unit (ICU). And some reporters who were on 'forced leave' on the premise that there wasn't so much demand for wide effort on story collection, were among those suspected to have been leaking information of the happenings to 'enemies' of the company.

M'membe's Post was seen by many in the public as a newspaper that fought so hard for the promotion of freedom of expression and a free press. But it is depressing as we noted that our rights as employees to express ourselves were often infringed upon. The paper didn't have room for employees to talk about delayed salaries or injustices perpetrated by some 'petty' managers, except during 'Muppet Shows' that were convened to act as though free speech was tolerated. And ironically, the newspaper instead had all the time to carry stories of other company employees' delayed payments and questioned why those entities delayed to pay what was owed to workers, and questioned why some public officers were allergic to divergent views, the views that even *The Post* itself didn't entertain to see the light of the day.

Those that did exercise their freedom of expression were shown the door through the company's infamous clause 4, a release clause which provided that management could terminate an employee's contract without giving reasons. Many faced the wrath of clause 4 and had no recourse once they received it.

M'membe was immovable when it came to being advised on issues relating to the management of his Post. If anyone advised him on a decision in the best interests of the company, his reply would be "I have been doing this for a long time, so what are you telling me, boss? If you want to do that, go and start your own company."

That is how he ran his 'empire'. Even in 2011 when he decided to extensively cover Michael Sata and the Patriotic Front (PF), he behaved the similar way.

In the run-up to the 2011 general elections, M'membe and *The Post* indirectly endorsed Sata, the main opposition candidate, against then Republican President Rupiah Bwezani Banda.

M'membe, through *The Post*, had on several instances accused judges and other public officers in government today, of being cadres; but, himself too was somewhat a PF supporter under President Michael Sata's government. Even his friends, who were appointed into government positions then, were staunch supporters of late President Sata's government. The fact is, even those that will be appointed as solicitor general, attorney general, or director of public prosecution, defense commanders, head of the intelligence, in subsequent governments are those that are loyal to whoever shall be in power, a trend that has proved consistency in Zambia today. So some cries do not hold water.

The Post published the positives about Sata in the run-up to 2011 elections, while on the other hand subjected Banda to ridicule. This proves he was a staunch supporter, or perhaps *The Post* as a whole, was; so why is he hating on those who are cadres for the PF today?

Shortly after president Levy Mwanawasa had been re-elected in 2006, he appointed Banda as his vice-president.

Banda's appointment received mixed feelings. Banda was a former United National Independence Party (UNIP) member who once held various diplomatic posts under the regime of Kenneth Kaunda. Those that failed to conceal their displeasure at Levy's choice for a vice-president spoke through the media. Topping that list of critics was M'membe's Post. According to him editorials in *The Post*, Rupiah Banda was a failure.

And so, because of M'membe's arguments on Banda's alleged incapacity to govern, an indirect war was declared. In June 2008, president Levy Mwanawasa suffered a stroke in Egypt and died in France five weeks later. Banda became acting Republican President.

During the mourning period, the PF of Michael Chilufya Sata, the UPND of Hakainde Hichilema, and the ruling MMD, under Banda's leadership, began their processes of selecting a candidate to contest the election to replace Mwanawasa as required by the Constitution.

Inevitably, despite interest shown by several long-serving members of the party, the MMD chose Banda as its candidate for the elections. However, this did not please those that managed *The Post*. Their preferred candidate was then Finance minister Ng'andu Magande, as was alleged by Rupiah Banda. The PF chose Sata while the UPND settled on Hichilema.

In the run-up to that election, *The Post* garnered it's sophisticated consignment of Rupiah Banda critiques and continued its campaign against Banda. However, against all odds and despite Sata's heated protestations about the election results, the Electoral Commission of Zambia declared Banda as the duly elected Republican President. *The Post* under the stewardship of M'membe, however, continued to 'unbundle' a continuous set of propaganda against President Banda. This resulted in M'membe facing contempt charges after he allegedly defied a ban of not printing "libelous" articles about the then MMD presidential candidate (later President) Rupiah Banda, in July 2011.

One chilly morning, MMD supporters, unhappy with the newspaper's coverage of their leader, marched to State House to seek the President's audience over what they termed "unprofessional reporting" and "non-remittance of taxes" by *The Post*. Rupiah Banda addressed the protestors and promised that he would 'ensure that *The Post* is closed'—as the newspaper put it in its headline.

"...They [The Post] started attacking me even before I became presidential candidate for the MMD; they continued attacking me up to now. I decided to fire Magande, who was their preferred candidate and you rejected him [Magande], because I have documents that he [Magande] wanted them [The Post] to go scot-free with the money they owe the Zambian people; that's why I fired Magande," Rupiah Banda, then as head of state is quoted to have said, in *The Post* edition of February 26, 2009.

"...we don't run a jungle government and I have been quiet for too long but this is the time to be vigilant and face them [The Post] head-on...as long as I continue to be President of this country, I will ensure that The Post pays back the debt they owe the Zambian people," ends excerpt from *The Post* newspaper.

So, the fight waged on. M'membe and his Post newspaper was not at any given time intimidated by the President's statement. And for sure, nothing happened. M'membe eventually won that battle; at least, for the time being.

But how, you may ask, did a journalist win a battle against the Head of State? Let's put it this way; Sata and the PF won the 2011 general elections and if you connect these events, you will recall that he received favourable coverage from *The Post* before and after elections. In effect, the PF 'owed' its victory to the 'mighty' *Post*.

At the announcement of PF's electoral victory in September 2011, wild celebrations took place on Bwinjimfumu Road as hundreds of jubilant students and PF supporters thronged the newspaper's head office, chanting slogans and thanking *The Post*.

At that moment, everyone thought that the means had justified the end. Everyone on the streets seemed to be celebrating the end of the MMD's 20-year rule.

Furthermore, President Michael Sata came into office. He became a darling of *The Post*! During his tenure, he hardly ever seemed to do anything wrong in the newspaper's eyes. *The Post* covered almost all of Michael Sata's ministers. They were darlings of the newspaper. This relationship and influence M'membe was believed to have built up with president Sata's clique led to the birth of what people started referring to as the 'Bwinjimfumu government.' M'membe was believed to have been controlling President Sata. It was said that appointments made in Sata's government had to be approved by M'membe before they were announced. And this led to M'membe and some in the PF being described as a cartel.

The so-called 'cartel' was a powerful clique. It supposedly comprised the likes of then Director of Public Prosecutions (DPP) Mutembo Nchito, his brother and lawyer Nchima Nchito, M'membe, former justice minister and PF secretary general Wynter Kabimba, former tourism minister Sylvia Masebo, former Attorney general Musa Mwenye, former Vice-president Dr Guy Scott and several of the late Sata's ministers.

As opposition leader, Sata had fought for over 10 years to become Republican President. I state with grief, however, that he did not enjoy the presidency. Poor health later into his brief presidency left him frail.

Sata, an outgoing leader and genuine people's person, began to disappear from public eye for several months, raising concerns among the citizenry about his health.

And because Sata had many seemingly sharp handlers, among them,

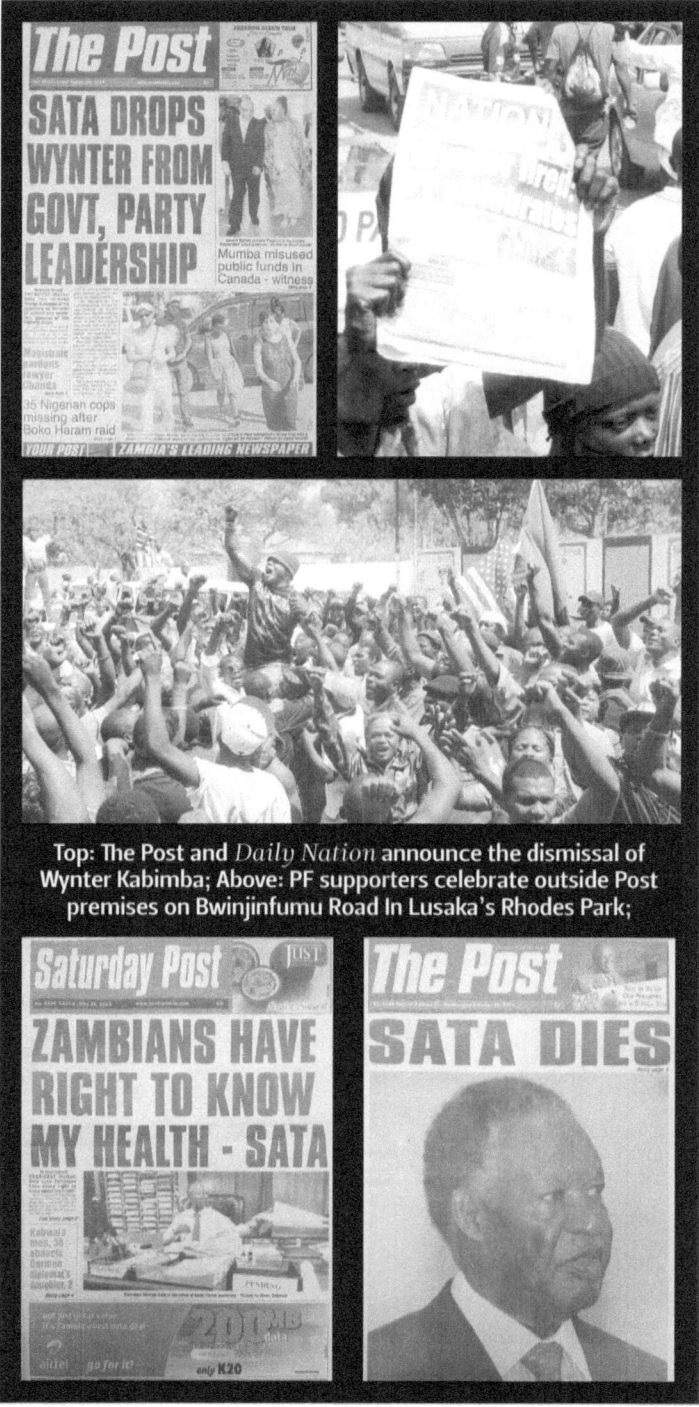

Top: The Post and *Daily Nation* announce the dismissal of Wynter Kabimba; Above: PF supporters celebrate outside Post premises on Bwinjinfumu Road In Lusaka's Rhodes Park;

former Post journalist George Chellah, as his press aide, a Facebook page was opened for the ailing President. This marked the commencement of Sata's 'Facebook rule or misrule,' if you like.

It was through Facebook that the Head of State 'managed or mismanaged' the affairs of the country. He had regular postings on what he had done, whom he had sworn in as what, among others. The strategy was to keep Mr Sata away from cameras. No journalists, except in a few instances where reporters from the Zambia News and Information Services (ZANIS), were allowed to film 'special assignments' the President had at State House.

How does this connect to the subject at hand, you may be asking? Well, while people that put President Michael Sata into office were curious to know what was happening to their leader, the once critical and independent newspaper, *The Post*, kept quiet, and 'secretly spoke' with Michael Sata who used to tell them he was fine and working. However, *The Post* knew that Michael Sata was not well like his ministers did. Someone once asked me, 'were such actions in the best interest of the people?' Well, this is my answer:

The PF of Michael Sata did not honour many of the promises it made to the Zambian people in the run-up to the 2011 polls. These promises included jobs for the youth, a turn-around in the economy within 90 days and resolving the 1964 Barotseland Agreement. The party also promised to release the new Constitution in a few days, that taxes were going to be low and that there was going to be more money in people's pockets.

The 90 days elapsed; there was no promise actualised! Assurances started coming from government on how committed it was to developing the country and how hurriedly, for that matter. After a year, people started calling for the Constitution, which the Sata regime had promised to deliver. Criticism began to grow.

But *The Post*, previously known for its never ending scuffles with governments owing to business and 'public' interests, did not carry anything that sounded like criticism against the PF or Michael Sata.

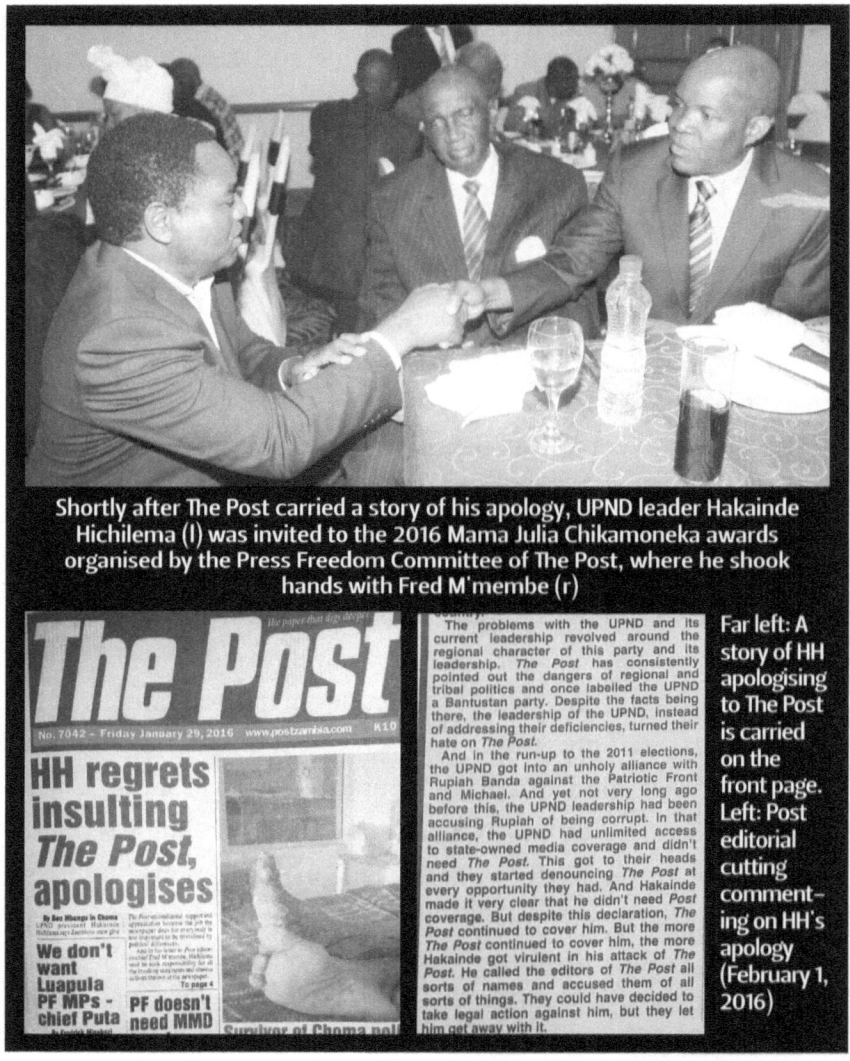

Shortly after The Post carried a story of his apology, UPND leader Hakainde Hichilema (l) was invited to the 2016 Mama Julia Chikamoneka awards organised by the Press Freedom Committee of The Post, where he shook hands with Fred M'membe (r)

Far left: A story of HH apologising to The Post is carried on the front page. Left: Post editorial cutting commenting on HH's apology (February 1, 2016)

Hichilema, who until 2016 was under a Post 'blackout', never had a platform to critique the PF as was expected of an opposition political party.

Reader, a comical fact you must note here is that; M'membe, whose reasons for his then stand-off with tycoon Hichilema remains speculative, a few days after a bullet pierced into The Post Newspapers' newsroom, ran away from the latter who visited the office to offer solidarity. At a time M'membe was informed that the opposition leader, Hichilema, had visited the paper's headquarters, he was in his then news-editor's office—the office he later left hurriedly, to avoid being noticed by the opposition leader who took time to interact with reporters in the main newsroom. When M'membe snubbed Hichilema, he rushed to the production department where he hid himself from Hichilema. Why he conducted himself this way, remains a mystery to those of us that witnessed it unfold.

Hichilema visited The Post Newspapers to get first hand information from reporters on the bullet that landed the newsroom. During this period, M'membe and Hichilema's stand-off had not yet been resolved. And according to M'membe, Hichilema was in the wrong; however, no reasons were given. So, in line with his practice, M'membe wanted Hichilema to write him a letter of apology.

However, even when he accepted UPND president Hakainde

Hichilema's apology, it was clear his 'forgiveness' was not genuine. All he wanted was to have Hichilema who had a following, to help him fight President Edgar Lungu in the 2016 elections. And therefore, the reconciliation between the two men was cosmetic. Hichilema wanted a platform to advertise himself, and M'membe wanted to ride on Hichilema's popularity to fight Mr. Edgar Chagwa Lungu.

Word had it in The Post Newspapers' corridors that, Hichilema once sought peace with M'membe, but, the editor-in-chief rejected his good gesture by tearing into tiny pieces, his 'peace-seeking' letter. However, Hichilema never seemed to have given up on the path of seeking peace, so in 2016, he gave it another 'shot', and boom, eureka! Peace was restored, and the paper carried a story quoting the tycoon's letter.

"*Over time, it is clear at least from my view that the relationship between you and I has be strained. This is in someway and at times can also be said to be the case between the United Party for National Development and The Post Newspapers Limited...*

"*In recognition of the above and in our desire to correct the situation, we state as follows: I take responsibility for those statements and actions which angered you, your family and The Post. I tender my apology to you, family and The Post for statements and actions*", read part of Hichilema's letter of apology to M'membe and *The Post*.

So, any story outside praising Sata was trashed. *The Post* ignored all those that had complaints against the PF. All it tolerated were praises for Michael Sata's government and in intervals, the paper gave priority to sex-scandal stories in society. *The Post* turned a blind eye to the pressing economic issues that needed the government's intervention.

Now, from the above, do you think this was all done in the best interests of the people? Did the means justify the end? Are the actions above a cause of public's lack of sympathy when *The Post* was facing closure? That is for you to judge.

The Post did all this to safeguard its own business interests; in this view, it abandoned the interests of the people it had stood for in 2011. So let's see what next happened to the PF and *The Post*.

At the time of all this propaganda for Sata-led government by *The Post*, M'membe's close ally Wynter Kabimba, then secretary general of the ruling PF party and justice minister, was busy touring provinces, 're-organising' the party. He removed provincial party officials Mr Sata had appointed, alleging that they were destabilising the party. He installed those he thought were 'good' for the party. After President Sata, Kabimba was the most powerful person in the party and government.

Kabimba, did not, however, remove PF officials for what he termed 're-organising the party'; he did it to destabilise Sata's PF party structures. Remember, Sata was ailing when all this was going on.

Kabimba has denied destabilising or creating parallel structures in the PF. Speaking on Millennium Radio's The Interview programme on April 5, 2017, he said, "I never did that and look, at what point do you even connect with those parallel structures. At what point do you do that? As secretary general, you can only work with the existing structures to the political party to which you belong. Those parallel structures were in people's imaginations. They did not exist."

Meanwhile, many other PF officials also lined up to take over the presidency after Sata. These included Geoffrey Bwalya Mwamba, popularly known as gbm, Chishimba Kambwili, former first lady Dr Christine Kaseba, Sata's son Mulenga, in-law Robert Sichinga, Wylbur Simuusa, Miles Sampa and Edgar Lungu.

In 2014, President Sata's health seemed to have failed him. He was constantly unwell and so, it was alleged that some people within the PF government connived and created email accounts purporting to have housed some alleged corruption of some officials.

And, although the official letter of dismissal issued to Kabimba by President Sata did not bear reasons why he was fired, it was speculated that former finance minister Alexander Chikwanda and others teamed up to have Kabimba pushed out of the way to the presidency. Kabimba was fired on August 28, 2014.

That day will remain historic to some of us that witnessed it unfold. It was a sad day for *The Post* and a happy day for those that had presidential ambitions in the PF. Wild celebrations broke out in several parts of the country. Some PF members in Lusaka marched to *The Post* on Bwinjimfumu Road carrying a coffin bearing Kabimba's name. They stood outside the entrance to *The Post*, chanting slogans.

At the time, M'membe was busy wrapping up that day's work – newspaper designing and editorial writing. When he heard the noise outside, he went to the gate, which was closed, and pulled out a pistol and fired one shot in the air. But instead of leaving, the cadres outside began cheering. Eventually, however, they noisily marched away from *The Post*.

Thus, ended Kabimba's ambitions for the PF presidency.

Edgar Lungu, a lawyer, during the Kabimba saga, rose from being deputy minister in the Office of then Vice-President Guy Scott to become home affairs minister and then defence minister after GBM resigned. And when Kabimba was fired, President Sata appointed Edgar Lungu as justice minister as well as PF secretary general, leaving Kabimba an ordinary party member. Interestingly, Lungu and Kabimba were classmates in the School of Law at the University of Zambia (UNZA) in the 1980s.

It is constitutional in Zambia that when the Head of State is leaving the country, he/she appoints someone to act as President in his absence. In October 2014, when President Sata was scheduled to travel to London, he appointed then defence and justice minister Edgar Lungu as acting president.

On October 28, Sata, died in a London hospital.

Almost immediately, the succession battles in the PF began. Edgar Lungu was still acting as president. And Vice-President Guy Scott was constitutionally barred from contesting the Republican presidency on the basis of his parentage. However, as vice-president, it was Scott's duty to preside over a three-month transitional period prior to the elections of a new president.

Stories topping the list in Post corridors at this moment alleged that M'membe and his 'cartel' friends were looking to find a way of having Kabimba contest the PF presidency and eventually the Republican presidency. But this proved an exercise in futility. Kabimba did not make it.

And in the PF, Edgar Lungu seemed to have been the favoured candidate. Nonetheless, he faced stiff competition from those that wanted to take over the presidency. Adding to the already long list of competitors was Dr Christine Kaseba. Just two days after the burial of her husband, the first lady declared her intention to join the race, whoever misled her. However, she was roundly criticised for 'abrogating mourning' tradition for the sake of wanting the presidency. So she, too, eventually failed. Edgar Lungu, banking on party's 'popularity' and cunning members, at a PF conference in Kabwe, ascended to the PF presidency.

Propaganda against then PF aspiring president Edgar Lungu never ran dry in *The Post* at a time when party membership was 'dying' to field the 'Chosen One'. M'membe called Lungu—his former lawyer—a drunkard and a swindler, whom he accused of squandering a client's legal fees.

Wherever this standoff came from, it's none of our business. M'membe's Post had declared 'war' against Edgar Lungu. And when Lungu eventually won the PF presidency, outsmarting the cartel, he too declared 'war' against tax defaulters. And so the fight raged on.

And in his letter to *The Post* and M'membe, then Zambia Revenue Authority Commissioner General, Berlin Msiska said, "*As you're aware in October 2011, we approved your appeal for a waiver of penalties and interest after you successfully paid the principal taxes in installments. Our expectations were that you would be a compliant taxpayer. However, it has come to our attention that you have accumulated another tax liability. You neglected to remain current with your tax obligations and accumulated yet another tax liability...*"

So now, due to a prolonged legal battle between ZRA and *The Post*, a ruling was delivered in 2016 in favour of ZRA. At this time, *The Post* debt had allegedly risen to about K53 million. In June 2016, ZRA moved in to recover the argued amounts and owing to lingering disputes between the newspaper and the tax authority on the size of the debt, the company was closed.

The company was said to have relaxed on remitting tax.

Let's ask ourselves again; were the actions by *The Post* not to report anything negative about President Sata and his government done in public interest? Did the ends justify the means? It's a small 'no' and big 'YES'. A big YES because *The Post* lost its vision in pursuit of good business deals. And a small 'no' because its intention was excellent but the execution and end result, portrayed a bad picture on their part. And for this, the company has been judged to have extensively covered the PF for its business interests. They wanted to avoid tax commitments, some people alleged.

In 2014, then finance minister Alexander Chikwanda, whose relationship with *The Post*, had soured at the time, was accused of having influenced ZRA to press the newspaper to pay its debt; at least an audio recording according to the newspaper, confirmed the minister's intentions. You must, however, note that Chikwanda is a distant relative of M'membe.

The question of objectivity is a very cardinal one. Let's deal with these questions that follow for us to appreciate the situation President

Edgar Chagwa Lungu and Dr Fred M'membe found themselves in.

If you were President Edgar Lungu and all Fred M'membe's Post newspaper published/reported was ridicule, 'insults', among other negative stories about you (without even five per cent positive ones), would you not have empowered ZRA to collect monies they owed?

Before we lose track, let's bring in President Lungu's perspective.

When it was reported that diplomats were calling on government to immediately re-open *The Post* saying the timing for shutting it was irrational and suspicious, the President who was on a 'busy' campaign trail, briefly halted his tours and called for a meeting at State House where he challenged diplomats to tell him the good timing for collecting revenue.

Even though the fact is that *The Post* owed ZRA, the tax authority's insistence on closing this critical newspaper so as to realise monies, came at a time when concerned citizens would attribute the company's closure to the PF's bid to be re-elected at all costs. Of course, Post Newspapers Limited needed to pay that which it owed the authorities. The company needed to be an example to other institutions it reported about. And may be the PF, which once received positive coverage from the paper, feared that had the newspaper remained open, the election was going to slip through its hands.

Let us halt being hypocritical or naive here. *The Post* bit a larger chunk it could not chew and it never considered objectivity or impartiality in its reportage. It merely launched a war against the 'big leagues'. Many issues it reported on were of its interest and not the interest of the majority Zambian people. As *The Post*, we were biased and we wanted glory to always come our way. But life is not like that!

In this practice, you give recognition where you see positives, critique and advise where you see wrongs. The journalism profession must not always target to remove an incumbent or always protect the incumbent; the profession should exist to benefit society, you, and the environment you are operating in.

So, hiding behind opinion rights to tell off your 'political' opponent, insulting them, does not represent the people's interests but your own selfish motives. No matter the rights one may have to hold their own opinions, maintaining sobriety in attempting to resolve issues is of great importance for the benefit of our motherland Zambia.

M'membe is not perfect; he has done the worst things as well as the best things and therefore, in many of his actions against his 'political' opponents, he needed to bear something in mind; that everyone is prone to error. But as a people, we must always strive to be better and not be comfortable with being error-prone.

Well, getting back to the question on what you would have done had it been you in President Edgar Lungu's shoes, holding a 'long-stick' and waking up with a face smeared with worst criticism by *The Post*; well this is a DEMOCRACY! And in a democracy, there is freedom of speech and as a leader, one can only learn when their deeds and decisions are critiqued; one must always be challenged when wrong is done and praised when right is done.

In simple terms, the ZRA, after being 'empowered' to collect money from business by President Lungu, should have given *The Post* newspaper an opportunity to pay and remain open. But also, if M'membe and *The Post* were up to saving the company from closure, they would have paid what ZRA claimed and later battle to reconcile the figures—something they so much wanted. However, closing down the newspaper robbed of government, huge sums of money in taxes; and the only people that benefited from it were those that felt *The Post* was standing in their way to 'successes'.

Did ZRA succumbed to pressure from the government to allegedly 'inflate' figures that The Post owed them or the latter forgot how much it owed the tax authority? Or perhaps ZRA's interests were not to collect money from *The Post* but to have it shut for good so they could sell property and realise some money.

If you ask them, thousands of kwachas in taxes were lost as a result closing *The Post*. The hundreds of employees that were rendered jobless after the closure of *The Post* were all taxpayers. Had the ZRA compelled the paper to pay its debts—with penalties—over a specified period, it would have cleared it by now, and the government would have 'more money in its pockets'.

The ZRA shut-down *The Post* and the newspaper claimed that procedure was not followed. Blame for the fall of *The Post* fell on the PF government. But government publicly denied having had a hand in the closure of M'membe's Post. It was speculated that this was all done to get at M'membe, who had proved to be a thorn in their way to several terms in power. However, today some people take the speculation as the "gospel truth" on what led to the closure of *The Post*.

There's an opinion that former president Rupiah Banda, who had once promised to collect debt from *The Post* in 2008, had backed Edgar Lungu's campaign in order to achieve that goal and to also make M'membe cry as he (Banda) did when he lost the 2011 elections to the PF of Michael Sata. M'membe has learned a lot of lessons from this ordeal. Who wouldn't?

The Post's closure certainly excited many of M'membe's perceived enemies, among them, Richard Sakala, the editor-in-chief of the *Daily Nation*. Sakala served a three-year jail term following a conviction for corruption and motor vehicle theft during his time as press aide to President Frederick Chiluba. Sakala believed that M'membe, using his Post, pushed for his conviction. For that reason, the 'demise' of *The Post* can be said to have excited him.

M'membe wanted what he desired to almost always go his way; but definitely not with the Edgar Lungu's regime that was determined to realise debt owed to the government. These guys had an 'independent' thought, and were more 'clever' than the people he had dealt with before.

The Post injured a number of people, some 'deserved it' and some did not. However, little was it known that M'membe's company, *The Post*, was a nest where the vultures that ultimately ate him were groomed!

But in Zambia today, no one can attempt to match their journalistic prowess to M'membe. His journalistic and entrepreneurship skills have almost no match in this country. M'membe must be celebrated, despite his flaws, like anyone of us.

He co-founded the Weekly Post after abandoning his well-paying accountancy job to start up a media house in the wake of the return to multipartism. The editorial policy of the Weekly Post was drawn up in February 1991 and the first edition of the paper hit the streets on July 26 of that year.

It's worth noting at this stage that when the MMD was formed in 1990, M'membe's uncle, Arthur Wina, was the Movement's interim leader. So, when the MMD held a convention at the Mulungushi International Conference Centre in Lusaka in early 1991 to select its candidate to challenge Kenneth Kaunda in the presidential election scheduled for later that year, Wina was defeated by Frederick Chiluba, a trade unionist. Chiluba polled about 62% leaving Wina with 19%, while the other candidates shared the remaining vote. It is alleged that M'membe grew bitter after Wina lost to Chiluba, he and hated him for that. In the MMD then, one had to poll 51 and above to be president of the party.

And following his election as party president and subsequently as Republican President, Chiluba appointed veteran journalist Richard Sakala as his press secretary. Over the years, Chiluba's schemes and 'corrupt' practices started being exposed in the Weekly Post (and later *The Post*) and that is believed to have ignited the tension between the newspaper and the MMD of Frederick Chiluba.

Having looked at the possible reasons that led to the bad relations between the newspaper and the politicians, let's get back to the reason we are here; summarising how the government closed *The Post*.

M'membe raised the newspaper profile to international standards with his critical stance against almost all regimes that 'abandoned' the interests of the people, at least according to him.

When *The Post* was closed, Fred M'membe and the company's managers were 'depressed', for this meant that many employees were to lose their jobs. They said President Edgar Lungu did not have a heart for the hundreds of employees that were rendered jobless the time the company was closed. By creating employment for hundreds of people, he became a hero to many. And to some, he was this brilliant journalist that used his employees to his advantage as most decisions made were in his own interests.

A handful of sympathisers from all walks of life regularly visited the 'open air' newsroom' to offer solidarity with the affected workers.

So, the question is, did Fred M'membe really care for his employees' well-being as he often said?

Well, if M'membe did care, why did he sometimes divert money meant for workers' salaries to his business expansion projects? There is still no rational explanation as to why this was done, who had powers to authorise payment of salaries, sometimes hesitated to do so despite the good business environment the company enjoyed. If Fred, as he preferred to be referred to, cared for employees, he would have directed the many unpaid loans to contracted from banks, to settling ZRA debt. This simple action would have saved our jobs, and therefore, without this, claims of caring for employees cannot be believed.

Despite working abnormal hours at *The Post*, we often went months without pay and the reasons given to us were that, the company was trying to clear-off revenue debt owed to ZRA; when it came to our attention that ZRA was after the company for the disputed amounts, our jaws literally dropped.

Many were the times during the company's monthly meetings (Muppet Shows) when M'membe gave assurances that there would be improvements in the way our affairs were going to be attended to. But the meetings served as nothing. If you interviewed most former Post employees today, they would tell you that M'membe valued more, his personal interests and not the interests of his workers that helped make *The Post* become what it became. So, when reading and hearing about M'membe's claims over his 'concern' for his former employees, not only irks former employees, but sometimes leaves them spooked!

In fact, a day after the tax authority's first attempt to close the company failed, while in a 'diary meeting'; we expressed concern over the threats to 'shut' the paper, but, we were given the impression that, 'the company had cleared all debt'. They further told us that, our salaries were delayed because the company was pressed to settle ZRA debt. Now, when the company was closed, the truth that was hidden from us, came out bare before our eyes and ears.

Instead of paying workers who at times went unpaid for several months despite the paper making 'a lot of money', M'membe bought a fleet of trucks as well as radio station equipment, among many of his business expansion projects (all this property has since been repossessed and some of it auctioned by ZRA in a bid to 'recover' its tax debt). Expanding one's business is one thing but asking employees to sacrifice so you can expand your business which they may not benefit from is another.

On a monthly basis, *The Post* made an average of K3 million in newspaper sales and advertising (and that is even before monies from other avenues could be added to the figures). Why it 'failed' to pay taxes remains a mystery to many, and why it closed with so much unpaid bank loans, remains more like a mythical tale.

The Post indeed mismanaged itself. M'membe's immovable attitude sunk what he had worked for, for over 25 years. M'membe as a major shareholder had a lot of lessons to learn from the downfall of his tabloid.

It is, however, gratifying to share with you that M'membe himself acknowledged that a lot of mistakes were made in the management of the company. His managers that took humble workers for granted and frustrated them; were often handed resignation letters, as workers were no longer able to stomach the 'drama' M'membe promoted in his company. Others simply left to explore new career paths. Reporters and other employees that gave objective opinions risked being labelled as traitors.

But despite his weaknesses and shortcomings, M'membe is a man who needs to be recognised and celebrated while he is alive. He has done a lot of good for his country; his contribution cannot be ignored. To me, Fred M'membe's Post gave me an opportunity to grow my career.

The Post's mission statement and editorial policy states in part: "*Our political role is to question the policies and actions of the authorities and all those who wield or aspire to wield social, economic and political power over the lives of ordinary people. We shall aim to protect and promote the newly-emerging democratic political culture, in which the fundamental rights and freedoms of individuals are guaranteed, through campaigning on issues that arise from our own investigations, reporting and analysis*".

The mission statement further stated that management was going to ensure that the paper was run as a business. And although he may have over-stepped his boundaries and stepped on many 'corrupt' people's toes in running this critical paper, M'membe must not be crucified for all what happened. At least, he was truthful from inception.

So, M'membe has unusual courage and a fighting spirit that today's and future generations can emulate. He is a freedom fighter. M'membe is in a league of his own! Many, who were like him, are no more.

M'membe is no angel; he is, like many of us, prone to error. He has not done wrongs exceeding what you have done and for this, no one in this country has a right to neither curse nor raise a finger against this great soul of Africa. Long live comrade Dr Fred M'membe and long live free press.

Police brutality

"We have to have a police that first and foremost, respects the Constitution of our land. But what we are seeing with this [Zambia] police is that they are doing neither. They have chosen to be subservient to the party in government and by being so subservient, they suppress the rights of everybody else, including the opposition. We cannot continue in a democracy where we have a partisan police. Innocent people are killed by the police and recently, a member of parliament Garry Nkombo was refuelling at a service station and he was almost shot by a drunken police officer."

CHAPTER FOUR

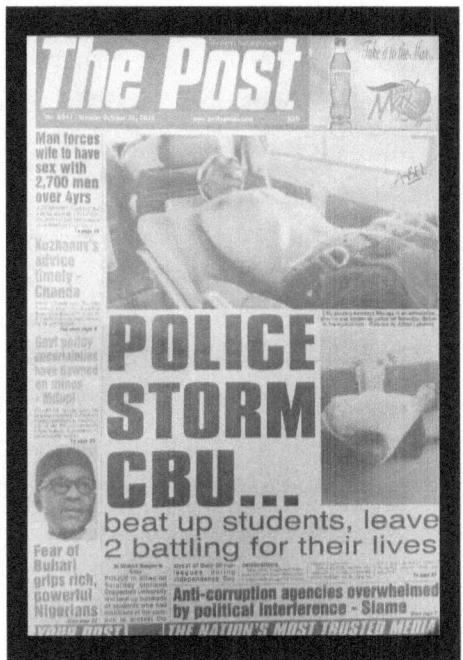

"...The police must be professional. They are not professional because a person who has been appointed to lead the police service has chosen to be a cadre of the PF, and that is Inspector General [Kakoma] Kanganja. You have failed us. If you're not capable, please resign, leave that position for professionals." These are the words of Charles Milupi, leader of the opposition Alliance for Democracy and Development (ADD) during a joint press briefing held at the UPND secretariat in Lusaka on March 28, 2017.

The high levels of unprofessionalism by our partners, the police, have always been an impediment not only to politicians but to a photojournalist whose duty is to inform, educate and entertain the masses.

The police are referred to as partners because they are the ones that ought to provide an environment of security for reporters doing their work in volatile and dangerous environments. This is not limited to reporters alone, the Constitution mandates the police to protect all citizens.

However, I pen these words with a heavy heart because many times the police, our partners, unfortunately see us as their number one enemy! This isn't supposed to be the case. Perhaps the Zambia Police Service, should include in its recruitment curricular the relationship officers ought to enjoy with the media as well as ordinary citizens, if it hasn't already.

The police command must know that this is not an era where the only skills you impart into your recruits are how to assault a perceived offender or how to assemble and fire a gun. Nor should it just be about how to hold a short baton or how to unleash pepper spray. This is a time to impart knowledge to all serving men and women in uniform—as well as potential recruits—on modern policing methods in the 21st century.

Equipping a police officer is more than just giving them riot gear. It also means equipping them with people skills to enable them to engage effectively with the public they serve as well as the media whose job it is to gather information and relay it to the masses.

Police brutality has long been part of our country's psyche. But to shrug our shoulders and continue to accept it, claiming that it has been there since the days of colonisation, would be tantamount to lunacy. It must end and it can only end if we highlight the challenges and provide solutions.

In the run-up to the 2016 general elections, the police's application of the Public Order Act was somewhat biased. This is a pre-independence law the PF had once promised to repeal once voted into office. They complained about it in the run-up to the 2011 general elections because the police under the MMD abused its application. However, after defeating the MMD that year, police under the PF began to abuse the same law.

Today, its the UPND who are crying foul over the 'unfair' application of the Public Order Act.

It is amazing to see media houses being shut under the PF regime because this is a party that enjoyed massive coverage by nearly all media outlets while in the opposition. It will go down in history that in 2016 the government, closed down The Post Newspapers through the ZRA, and through the Independent Broadcasting Authority (IBA), suspended the broadcasting licenses of MUVI Television and Komboni Radio and that the government through the Zambia Police, arrested the entire Radio Mano staff in Kasama and harassed individual journalists.

When Komboni Radio was closed, the police brutalised its director Lesa Nyirenda. Lesa was almost stripped naked by overzealous police officers that were deployed to man the radio station after the IBA suspended its broadcasting license.

After being off-air for several weeks, the station begged for leniency and the IBA lifted the suspension. Lesa returned to the station where she found police who seemingly failed to understand that an order had been issued to re-open the station.

In her attempts to access the radio station's premises, six male police officers resorted to physically harassing the lone Lesa, ripping off her clothes in the process. She was left bedridden at the University Teaching Hospital (UTH), nursing injury from her encounter with belligerent police officers. She would, however, not be the last woman to be treated this way by Zambian security personnel.

On February 15, 2017, armed police officers stormed the home of M'membe with a view to arresting him. At the time, M'membe had travelled to Jamaica and the United States. The reasons for wanting to arrest M'membe were on allegations that he and lawyer Nchima Nchito, between December 2016 and February 2017 "masqueraded" as Post employee and lawyer respectively. In this case, the complainant was former Post journalist Abel Mboozi, again.

What is of interest in this discussion is the level of brutality exercised by the police in this matter. Upon receiving that complaint, the combined security personnel swooped in on M'membe's house and effectively occupied it.

This matter was given more urgency by the police service than they give other concerns reported to them by ordinary citizens. This move was condemned and labelled as a politically motivated move, hence the urgency it received. Critics of the PF said that there was so much crime that demanded the police's most efficient and not engineered arrests.

Government agencies must have been aware of M'membe's departure. But the police insisted that they enter his premises and arrest him. They resorted to using force after his wife Mutinta Mazoka M'membe allegedly resisted them. The police produced a search warrant but Mrs M'membe was later accused of having torn it. It was at this moment that police are said to have became physical; they roughed her up and arrested the 'poor' woman.

This may sound like a stunt. But it was all too real. Citizens in this country have wondered what benefit there may have been for the police to behave in the manner they did.

Zambia does not belong to individuals like M'membe, Hakainde Hichilema or Edgar Lungu; Zambia is every countryman and woman's land and therefore, the Zambia Police must work professionally for the people of this nation and not be seen to be serving a few individuals.

It has been observed with dismay that since independence, successive governments have used the police to deal with their perceived enemies. But what legacy do these people care to leave?

What our leaders must know is that they will not always be in office; their mandates expire and they could end up being victims of the same police brutality others are subjected to.

The Zambia Police will only become a service when its operations are independent. If the current police service system is not changed or repealed, suspicions of abuse of the service will not end.

An ex-con and the closure of *The Post*

Richard Sakala and his *Daily Nation* newspaper is another journalist who is accused of not being objective in his reporting. The opposition has criticised the *Daily Nation* and some have said it was working like vultures, awaiting a chance to pounce on its weak prey—M'membe and *The Post*.

Sakala must have choked with envy when *The Post* carried public relations stories for the PF and Michael Sata.

He wished he was in that position presiding over the institution that carried public relations services for the government of Sata, but alas, he wasn't. And when M'membe's Post newspapers couldn't stomach Edgar Lungu contesting the presidency, Sakala's newspaper took advantage of it and stood firm to extensively cover the 'chosen PF president' in the 2015 by-elections. And a relationship between the *Daily Nation* and the PF was established, an allegation Mr Sakala dispelled when speaking on a 5fm.

Previously, the *Daily Nation* reported on the alleged corruption in the PF government under Sata, as they also carried favourable stories of the opposition United Party for National Development (UPND).

President Sata's death saw the UPND being abandoned by the *Daily Nation*, they had now found a new friend in Edgar Lungu of the PF. Whatever prompted this newspaper to shift its allegiance from UPND to PF is a mystery!

Richard Sakala was President Frederick Chiluba's press aide from 1991 to 2001. On March 5, 2004, Sakala was sentenced to a total of 14 years with hard labour for abuse of authority of office and theft of a motor vehicle. However, after having served three years and four months, he was released.

"...I served my sentence because I was convicted under an offense that was not bailable. So, I could not go out. So I spent 3 years, 4 months, 20 days, 16 hours, in prison because I could not do anything about it. And I don't think that is correct, it's not correct. Anybody arrested must be able to challenge the validity of their arrest." Sakala said speaking on 5fm's the Burning Issue in July 2017.

In his book A Mockery of Justice, Sakala attempts to clear his name of the reasons he was 'falsely' convicted on. He alleges that his conviction was as a result of being framed by former Director of Public Prosecutions (DPP) Mutembo Nchito and his brother Nchima, former Post editor-in-chief Fred M'membe and late president Levy Mwanawasa through the Task Force on Corruption.

This chapter will not attempt to confirm or refute Sakala's claims, but to instead deduce reasons to what is happening today. Sakala complained that he was unjustly treated and that his subsequent conviction was predetermined by public opinions in the media like *The Post*.

Here is an excerpt from A Mockery of Justice: "*...with regime change in 2001 as President Chiluba gave way to President Levy Mwanawasa, an opportunity availed itself for the information to be offloaded to punish the offending leaders. This had to be done in the most effective manner possible, they decided to use the Post Newspaper*".

"*The Post newspaper was used to churn out propaganda against civil servants, politicians and judicial officers considered inimical to the interest of the Task Force, as a result, the irredeemable differences within the nascent Task Force grew wider and deeper, while the President's preference was clear. He wanted Dr Chiluba out of the national political equation using the propaganda offered by the Post newspaper.*"

Without doubt, one can deduce that Sakala formed his *Daily Nation* with a vision to one day exact revenge on the cartel—the Nchitos and M'membe. He believed that the only way he could fight them was to have 'propaganda tools'—a publication that would discredit them and help him ensure they too 'end up in jail'. He believed that *The Post* newspaper and M'membe had convicted him long before the courts could pass judgment.

On the other hand, Sakala seemingly believed that the formation of the *Daily Nation* could help pursue justice for all. But today it is clear as observed that his vision to one day get back at the Nchitos and M'membe has come to pass.

The similar thing that happened to Sakala and President Chiluba in *The Post* is almost the same thing that Sakala is doing to M'membe and the Nchito brothers using his *Daily Nation*.

As human beings, we often tend to forget that the things we do to others today can have a bearing in future. We forget that history has an uncanny tendency of repeating itself. When the 'campaign against corruption' was launched, M'membe and his Post, alongside the Nchitos, did not at any time think that their actions towards Sakala would return to haunt them one day. As the saying goes, "opportunity comes to all that wait."

Sakala waited for years for the moment when his 'propaganda tool'—the *Daily Nation*—would be in a position to sort out the cartel. The opportunity presented itself and today, his persecutors are tasting their own medicine.

The similar way that Fred M'membe and the Nchitos behaved during the Mwanawasa government is nearly the same way that Sakala is using his tabloid to fight those that 'sent' him to jail for over three years. Karma, it would appear, is at work.

It is said that when two elephants fight, it's the grass that suffers. Sakala's interest, in all of this, is to level vengeance on those that made his stay outside State House a living nightmare. Like M'membe, Sakala's interests are currently not the greater good of the nation, but for his business. These are businessmen who use their 'enmity' to sell newspapers.

These are men who seek public sympathy to better their enterprises. Sakala's interests are not to help better the living standards of the suffering Zambians, but to make 95 per cent profits while the other five per cent is for pretentious reporting for the people. But he must learn something from M'membe's fall from grace. It is things like what he is doing that brought about the fall of *The Post*. *The Post* 'created' many enemies in its fight against 'corruption' and indirect endorsements of politicians in power.

My hope as an enthusiastic journalist appreciating Sakala's contribution to media pluralism is what happened to him vis-a-vis *The Post*—Fred M'membe's relations should never replicate itself again in the history of Zambian media. The perceived vindictiveness may have been a misplaced view against M'membe, but who knows the real truth? It may have existed.

They say life is like a roller coaster; it has many tight turns and steep slopes. People ride it and it dramatically changes in manner as its movement is wildly unpredictable. Fred M'membe enjoyed his time on the higher side of life but today, he is on the slope.

Nothing lasts forever; so, what kind of example do our veteran journalists want to pass on? Is it a life of vengeance, hate and selfish interests at the expense of greater public interest? That is something that needs honest reflection.

If Zambian privately-owned media could, despite their publication's agenda and missions, work towards a common goal—that is holding those in leadership accountable, this sovereign State could one day boast of growth and a sharp decline in the ever-widening gap between the rich and the poor.

As things stand, we are all alive to the fact that politicians will almost always promise to do things for our people that they themselves understand would not do in reality. This is why we need a united media to hold politicians to account. The private media is the backbone of Zambia's future depending on how the private sector restructures operations.

Sakala, like M'membe, is a journalist with great skill and experience, coupled with an entrepreneurial mind that has, to some level, benefited this country. He deserves to be respected and honoured. He started the *Daily Nation* when there was a regime that did not entertain him as it did with M'membe. But because of his passion, he braved the storm and started it nonetheless. It has grown to what it is today because of his unwavering efforts to broaden the media industry.

M'membe, Kabimba and the formation of the Rainbow Party

For several months, M'membe, former Rainbow Party deputy general secretary, Dr Cosmas Musumali conducted week-long classes at *The Post* newspapers where they 'trained' some of the employees in socialism. At the end of the class, employees 'graduated' with certificates in Introduction to Socialism. In my class, the certificates were presented

CHAPTER FOUR

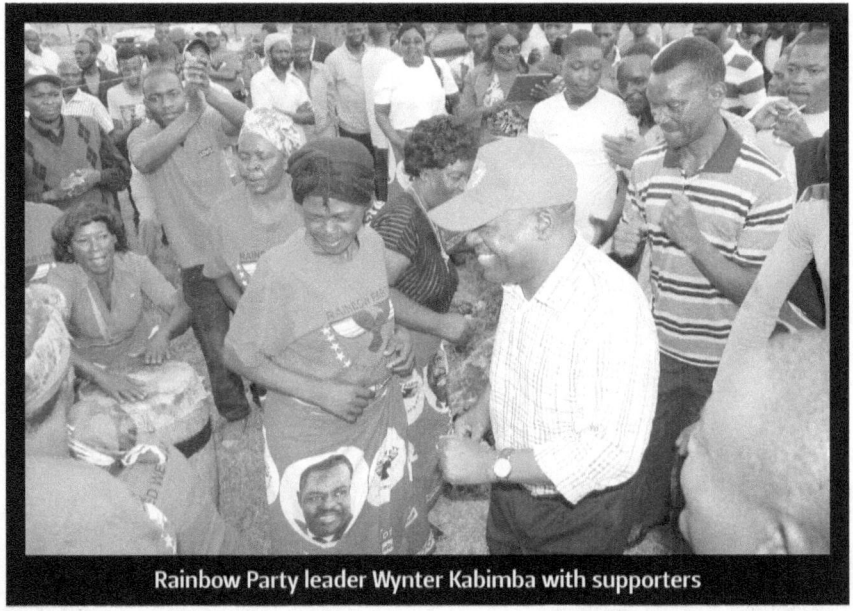

Rainbow Party leader Wynter Kabimba with supporters

to me and others by Rainbow Party general secretary Wynter Kabimba at our former printing offices off Lumumba Road.

My class was a privileged one; as we rubbed shoulders with renowned satirical artiste Pilato (Chama Fumba), among other non-Post workers that found the classes 'enlightening'.

You see, sugar-coating bitter and poisonous consumables can never make them taste sweeter nor less poisonous than they really are. Therefore, this book focuses on objectivity, impartiality, truthfulness and ethos.

This book is bare breasting truth without favouring or sweet-talking anyone. Remember that characters discussed in this book are of great importance to the journalism and political governance systems of this country. For us to understand The Untold Story of a Zambian Journalist, more journalism personalities and their contributions shall be told as below:

It is a fact that veteran journalist Fred M'membe is an influential personality in the annals of Zambia's media industry, as well as some other parts of the world. Dr M'membe may be said to have once had

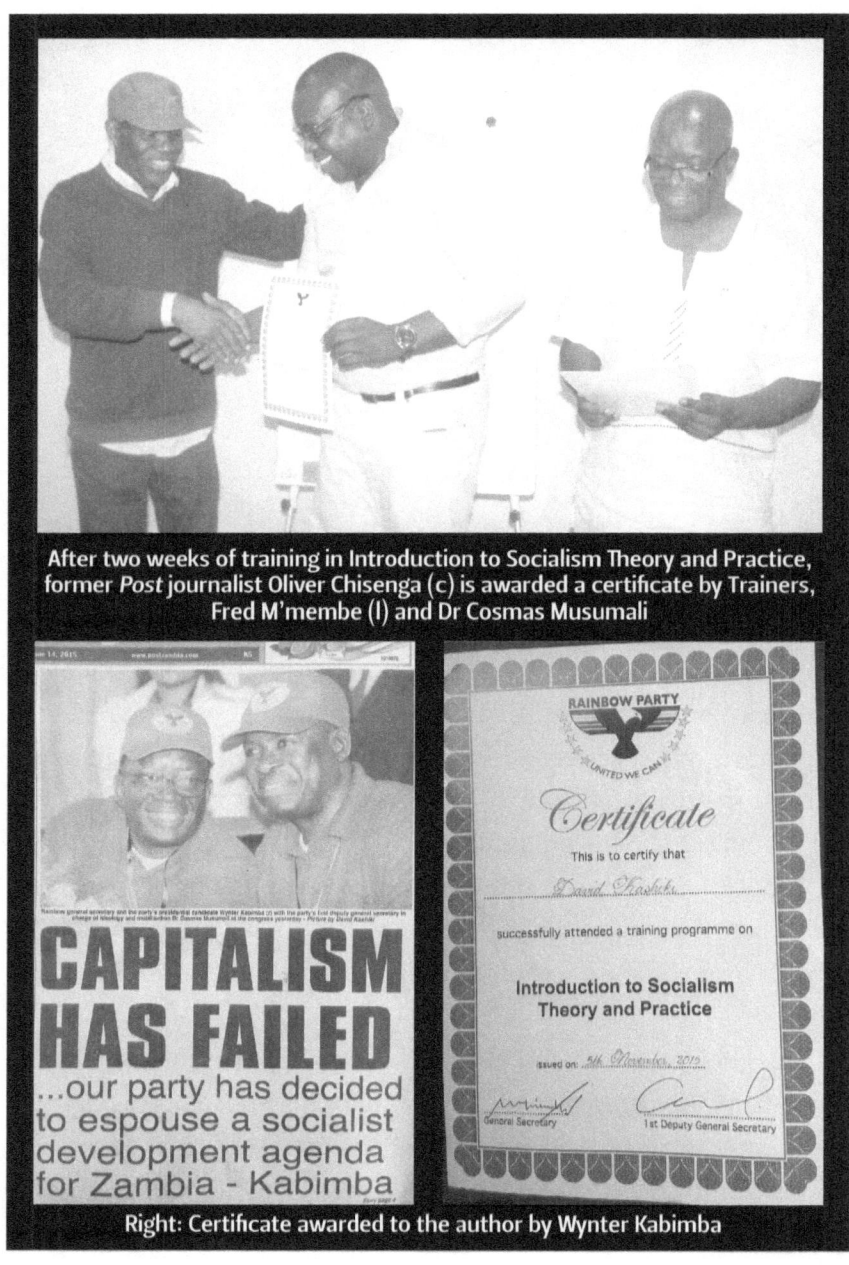

After two weeks of training in Introduction to Socialism Theory and Practice, former *Post* journalist Oliver Chisenga (c) is awarded a certificate by Trainers, Fred M'membe (l) and Dr Cosmas Musumali

Right: Certificate awarded to the author by Wynter Kabimba

well-meaning interests in most of his entrepreneurial endeavours. Another well-known fact about Dr M'membe is his love for renowned late Cuban revolutionary Fidel Castro and socialist ideologies he espoused.

CHAPTER FOUR

"And as for me, behold I establish My covenant with you and with your descendants after you, and with every living creature that is with you: the birds, the cattle and every beast of the earth with you, of all that go out of the ark every beast of the earth. Thus I establish My covenant with you: never again shall all flesh be cut off by the waters of the flood; never again shall their be a flood to destroy the earth". And God said: "This is sign of the covenant which I make between Me and you, and every living creature that is with you for perpetual generations: I set My rainbow in the cloud, and it shall be for the sign of the covenant between Me and the earth. It shall be, when I bring a cloud over the earth, that the rain shall be seen in the cloud", so said God to Noah in Genesis 9: 9 – 14.

And so, the rainbow scriptures in the Bible could be said to have inspired the formation of Wynter Kabimba's party. He had to hearten his followers mostly—PF rejects, with the name 'Rainbow' Party, which he hoped would in turn rejuvenate their hope for a 'just' society. This was Kabimba's covenant with those that bought into his ideas of forming a government in 2016 after he was flushed out of the PF inner circles in a manner that forced him into going 'underground' for numerous months.

The Rainbow Party, announced at Lusaka's Mulungushi International Conference Centre on December 16, 2014 by Kabimba, has or had ideologies premised on shrinking the gap between the rich and the poor in Zambia.

Kabimba had resigned from the PF soon after Sata's death and went underground to organise, with others, the formation of Zambia's first-ever democratic socialist party.

Tick School Day and Boarding was a hive of activity on June 26, 2015 when the Rainbow Party held its first general conference, where Dr Musumali was unveiled as first deputy general secretary. The site was a sea of red; women and men all dressed to the occasion. This day, for some of us that witnessed it, was a priceless moment in Zambia's political history.

After Kabimba and his then close friend M'membe fell from grace, the two are said to have sat down to brainstorm on the need to have a political party that would 'promote' equal distribution of wealth, provision of all basic necessities, and would restore order and sustain laws of this sovereign State once voted into power. To those that do not understand and know him, M'membe is not only a brilliant journalist but he is also a seasoned political strategist. Because of the socialism classes that were held at Post premises led to the belief that M'membe was part of the Rainbow Party.

Months before Kabimba called for a press conference where he announced the formation of the Rainbow Party, M'membe used to tell us and his close colleagues that there was still room in Zambia for the birth of a political party that would take a socialist approach and that would have the potential to change the way national affairs were being run. For M'membe and many others, the PF had failed to implement many of the policies enshrined in its manifesto.

So M'membe was largely believed to have birthed the idea of forming a political party with the then Wynter Kabimba. This was after alleged numerous attempts by the 'cartel' to persuade the 're-branded' PF, into fielding Kabimba—who at that time had remained an ordinary member of the party, to contest the PF presidency at the historic Kabwe Rock of Authority.

So did this group of 'revolutionists' really believe in what they had embarked on? Were these comrades really socialists? Well, like the saying goes, you can't judge a book by its cover!

At the face of all this controversy, Rainbow members frequented Post premises to either lunch or meet with their 'comrade'.

Rainbow members' heavy presence at the Post, made M'membe to be believe to be the mastermind of the idea to birth this socialist party. Rainbow Party officials frequented *The Post* offices, and this made reporters uncomfortable as their presence somehow signalled delayed pay.

The Post Newspapers soon became the quasi-headquarters for the democratic socialist Rainbow Party. All meetings relating to the party were often conducted and held at the newspaper offices until we reporters expressed concerns with M'membe during a diary meeting. In that meeting, we openly told him we were uncomfortable with him and Rainbow Party holding meetings at the newspaper offices. Our fear was that had any outsider known of this, we would all have been labelled Rainbow Party cadres and not professional journalists.

Youths, women and the old all visited The Post head offices to either lunch at the company's canteen or basically visit with the hope of being smeared with a few 'kwachas' by the party 'mastermind'.

Like a walk of a thousand miles to have safe drinking water, Kabimba's security detail too, at lunch time, walked from Lusaka's Godfrey House on Longolongo Road near Levy Park where they screened those that hoped to meet the democratic-socialist Rainbow Party leader, to The Post headquarters on Bwinjimfumu Road. Rainbow Party vehicles all refueled at M'membe's Post printing plant offices on Lumumba Road.

And most importantly, Kabimba was guaranteed of front page headlines each time he opened his mouth to speak as Rainbow Party leader. His pictures were flashed on the front page of *The Post* each time he was photographed. This was how far M'membe and Kabimba's friendship went. In fact, M'membe fielded two of his employees in the 2016 parliamentary elections in Mongu Central and Itezhi tezhi constituencies. The two got leave at the time of contesting.

Now, while addressing delegates at the first-ever general conference at Tick School in Lusaka on June 26, 2015, a confident Kabimba told the nation that his party would form government on August 11, 2016.

Hearing their leader's optimism and eloquence, Kabimba's supporters immediately picked up drums and sticks, buckets and chairs and made music to show their excitement. As this unfolded, Kabimba paused to catch a glimpse of how women and men danced joyously at the colourful event.

However, during the August 11, 2016 polls, Kabimba, the once perceived excellent mobiliser and great politician under the PF of Michael Sata, received a paltry 9,504 votes out of the 3,781,505 cast from the 156 constituencies in Zambia.

In the run-up to the elections, many of us working at The Post observed that the relationship between M'membe and Kabimba was deteriorating. Here is something you may not have known about the two men: Both were strong personalities and as we learned in Physics, like poles repel. M'membe and Kabimba do not accept to be pushed around anyhow. M'membe was believed to have attempted to control Kabimba on how to run the socialist party, but that was not to be. That was not Kabimba's style!

So, unable to reconcile their differences, the two men decided to go their separate ways. Kabimba soon stopped enjoying coverage in *The Post*.

Speaking on Millennium Radio's *The Interview* programme on April 5, 2017, Kabimba confirmed his relation with M'membe were on rocks by saying, "I have not seen or spoken to Fred [M'membe] since August 2016. Fred was not also a member of the Rainbow Party; he is not a member of the Rainbow Party."

Kabimba's running mate in the August 2016 election, Dr Musumali, who is Fred M'membe's close friend, resigned from the party shortly before vote tallying could be concluded by the Electoral Commission of Zambia. The Rainbow Party had started crumbling.

As we conclude this chapter, it is cardinal to note that the two men were close friends and that M'membe after having so much faith in Kabimba's leadership potential, decided to offer a platform on which the Rainbow Party could market its ideologies.

Before penning this chapter, I conducted research that showed that a number of journalists across the world have in some way or another funded political parties, raising questions about the impartiality, objectivity and ethos of such actions.

Many scholars have argued that it is ethically incorrect for a journalist to fund a political party because of the issues surrounding objectivity and impartiality. The concern here is how is it possible for a journalist who funded a political party or candidate to hold them accountable once they abuse authority? And if corruption was recorded, would the journalist report matters surrounding it with the impartially and objectivity it deserves?

Despite the potential for controversy, some journalists who have made political contributions reject the notion that their interests are conflicting, arguing their actions as private citizens and as journalists are not mutually exclusive.

Paul Tharp, a business reporter for the New York Post, in 2009 donated $750 towards the election campaign of former US Representative for New York's 13th congressional district, Michael McMahon, the Centre's analysis of Federal Election Commission records show. According to Tharp, as reported by *opensecrets.org*, he was satisfied with McMahon's public service and stated in his defence that he needed not to give up his rights simply because he was a reporter. He further stated that he had interest in public service, hence his donation.

There is need for the media to strive to strike a difference between governance activism and political activism. Many media outlets today have mistaken political activism for governance activism. So, in discussing the notion of journalists' political donations, the concern of a media outlet risking compromising its integrity or credibility must be raised.

For example, if your friend, spouse or any other relative announces their intention to run for public office, what is the best thing a media outlet or you as a journalist can do? The answer is simple: if you can report objectively with the impartiality demanded, there is nothing wrong with you handling that story. But if you can't, recuse yourself to avoid undermining the integrity of your media house. Knowing how difficult it is for one to not want to favour those they are emotionally attached to, however, the best thing would be to declare interest in the matter.

Media outlets that go against the laws and or ethics of journalism risk being perceived as political opponents by those they report negatively on in the news. This may be so because a particular media house may not report objectively on issues surrounding their relatives and non-relatives.

Like many have correctly observed, all journalists are human beings before they are reporters. Thus, they have personal convictions and ambitions. In a democracy, every person is free to decide to participate in the political affairs of their country. However, journalists should never use their profession as guise for pursuing their political ambitions.

As journalists, it is ethically wrong to publicly announce your support for any political party while you are still practicing the noble profession. When one feels they want to contest an election, telling people the truth may not hurt at all. It is always important to come out in the open and serve the people as a politician or revolutionist and there is nothing wrong with that.

Because of the alleged need to control Kabimba, towards the end of 2016, Post journalists were instructed not cover Kabimba and his party unless advised otherwise by the editors.

2016 saw most noted Rainbow members resign while Kabimba fired all those he believed were inclined to M'membe. However, the Rainbow Party's justification for the expulsions were centred on indiscipline and misappropriation of funds. Thus ended their 'socialist' relationship!

CHAPTER FIVE

Poor wages: A cause of compromised and unprofessional media

Have you ever sat down to imagine what poverty could do to you if it crept into your house? Have you carefully thought through what poverty-stricken families go through when they go minus a meal in a day? Well, they say people can only stomach so much.

In Zambia, the media is an ever growing and viable industry. Media houses are coming up regularly. This is coming at a time when journalism schools are equally producing a large number of journalists. But the problem in the media industry today is remuneration. Very few journalists in the country today get respectable salaries. Journalists barely survive to make ends meet despite the great service they do for society. But while journalism renders a great service to Zambia, that does not mean giving a service to the nation at no fee.

The very moment a student steps into a journalism class in Zambia, the warnings by lecturers of how the profession cannot give one a decent or modest salary, pops up. But the question is, in the near future, with the ever-increasing cost of living, will there be more people aspiring to be journalists in the country? This and many questions can be best addressed by media entrepreneurs who 'decide' to pay poor salaries to their workers.

Media owners in this country have at times deliberately made it a habit to pay their scribes meagre salaries because, 'they don't' make money.

Worth noting here is that privately-owned media houses, often times, grapple with generating income and so, it is not easy to pay journalists well. The private media, despite its best efforts, struggle to make money from advertising. This struggle is compounded with some politicians' intolerance to criticism.

When a radio station, newspaper or television station features a person that is perceived to be critical of the ruling party, those in authority tend to use government agencies to threaten and intimidate potential advertisers if they associate with them.

However, a blind eye should not be turned to this issue. Private media owners tend to become selfish even when they are making money; they channel their profits to other projects, starve their reporters of salaries for months and in the end, pay them peanuts. This leads to alarming levels of poverty among journalists and it is always a potential to compromise weaker souls.

Poverty knows no one; media entrepreneurs must know that when you don't pay your scribes for what they may have worked for, you are courting trouble. To begin with, your levels of professionalism fall sharply because your workers would have been bought off by politicians or organisations that want their news reported or not at all.

For the media to have a dedicated work force, there is need to remunerate scribes decently. If this important factor is ignored, the media will lose brilliant journalists that will in the end want to impress those in power in exchange for political appointments. Other scribes will even consider branching off into public relations where they hope to get a modest pay, enough to help sustain themselves and their families.

And below, is a statement issued by Panos highlighting the issues discussed in the passage above:

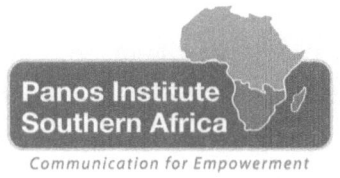

Press Statement

PSAf commemorates World Press Freedom Day, challenges journalists to be critical

Lusaka, 03 May 2017: Panos Institute Southern Africa (PSAf) today joins the world in commemorating World Press Freedom Day, a day set aside by the United Nations to celebrate and defend freedom of the media.

This year's commemoration is being held under the theme: *Critical minds for critical times: media's role in advancing peaceful, just and inclusive societies*. The theme is quite relevant to current and recent developments in some Southern Africa countries, where the media's efforts to advance peace, justice and inclusivity have faced hindrance. In any democratic dispensation, the media has a responsibility to be a critical mind, a watchdog that speaks truth to power and promotes accountability.

While the region has recorded an increase in the number of media establishments, PSAf is concerned that the media is falling short in its responsibility to be a critical voice for the region. We encourage journalists in the region to be strong amid various challenges, and be the critical voice that the region needs.

As we commemorate World Press Freedom Day, we are alive to the sad realities of Southern Africa's media sector which have resulted in the media failing to serve as critical minds for critical times. These include:

Threats and Harassment of Journalists: In the past year, we have recorded numerous cases of media practitioners in the region who have been harassed in their line of duty. These threats and harassment instil fear among journalists, causing them to be less critical and avoid any coverage that they feel could further expose them. Instead of advancing peace, justice and inclusivity, media practitioners are forced to avoid any content that may expose them. PSAf condemns all forms of harassment or threats against journalists. We will also continue to engage governments, political actors, civil society and other stakeholders to work together to ensure safety and security of journalists covering electoral processes.

Limited guarantees for freedom of the media: While countries in the region have varied media laws and varied media environment, the use of direct and indirect approaches to limit the influence and reach of the media seems to be a common denominator. Where freedom is not absolutely guaranteed, as is the case in most Southern Africa countries, it is difficult for the media to serve as critical minds in society. We commend countries like Malawi that recently enacted the Access to Information Law, which compels those holding public information to share it, and to some extent provides for protection of journalists. In the same vein, we encourage those countries—such as Zambia—that have been dilly-dallying on the enactment of the Access to Information and other press freedom laws to follow suit. When media freedom is guaranteed, critical journalism thrives.

Poor conditions of service for media workers: We are saddened to note that the conditions of service for media workers in some countries in the region remain bad and appalling at the same time. A lot of journalists work under very difficult conditions, and some go for months without salaries. Instead of focusing on their service to the public, media practitioners spend a lot of time worrying about where they will get money to meet some of their necessities. This makes them vulnerable to manipulation by whoever can dangle money or other benefits to them. It is difficult or impossible for a journalist to be critical when he or she is worried about how they would meet their basic needs.

The underlying effect of all these challenges is a dearth in investigative journalism and general decline in the standards of journalism, where the media is becoming less critical. This in turn affects the quality of content that millions of Southern Africa's citizens get from the media. When citizens are not adequately informed, their ability to be critical and hold their leaders to account is also affected. To address the declining standards of investigative journalism in the region, PSAf is currently supporting media practitioners with fellowships to produce content on development issues of local concern.

This World Press Freedom Day is an opportunity for all stakeholders to reflect on how they can contribute to making the media to be truly critical minds in critical times, advancing the region's socio-economic development.

Issued by:
Lilian Saka-Kiefer
Executive Director, Panos Institute Southern Africa (PSAf)
Email: general@panos.org.zm, **Tel:** +260 978 778 148/9

Zambia in dire need of youth leadership

Almost every politician today talks of how Zambia is in dire need of youth leadership. But you may wonder whether their concern is about 'irrational' leadership; the leaders that would not uphold the principles of democracy? If their answer is yes to the latter, ours as a rational youth is a no! Zambia is in need of leadership that is going to effectively and honestly lead posterity and today's generations.

President Edgar Lungu's critics have expressed displeasure at his choice for youth appointments into the public service as well as in his party structures. The President's decision to appoint youths, be it cadres or professionals in positions of high authority, deserves commendations.

I have come to learn in my few years of practicing journalism that most cadres in political parties exhibit leadership potential during their party's political activism activities. And it is from this point that higher party leadership sees who deserves a particular appointment at any level.

Any government is formed from a political grouping comprising the youth, women, men and the elderly. So, those that question presidents that appoint youths from their parties, what advice do you as critics put forth to help the appointing authority in hiring a competent crop of youths that would support their interests or agenda as a party in government?

Job on training is, however, an exception. It is irresponsible for someone to appoint youth or other cadres that do not understand anything about public affairs management into positions that require seasoned experts. The public service should not be used as a dumping site for youths that may not even understand its operations.

This is why there is need in African politics and Zambia in particular to seriously consider investing in the education of its youth cadres. When this measure is taken up, leaders will have a wide choice from which to appoint youths into government positions, among others. And the truth of the matter here is that no matter how much critics talk, it amounts to nothing for those in power as they have no option but to reward loyal party cadres that may share the same values and principles for their plans for the country, be it good or bad.

Every political party wants to reward its disciples. There may be no problem with that; but have the parties prepared an educated youth to take over the management of public affairs? Have the United Party for National Development (UPND), the Forum for Democracy and Development (FDD), United Progressive Party (UPP), People's Party (pp), Rainbow Party, etc started grooming their youth for future leadership roles? The country is in dire need of quality leadership. If these parties are doing so, then Zambia is headed for greatness.

And so, instead of critiquing with envy the position the PF is in, other political parties should formulate strategies that would help them impart skills in their youth followers today. Zambians are tired of empty talk and recycled-criticism. Political rhetoric must be removed from this country's social and political dispensation if we are to meet our estimated developmental goals.

This can be made possible if the media in this country fosters debate and campaigns to give a platform to young emerging leaders. Most statements covering newspaper pages are made by older politicians but this must not always be the case. Youths must be accorded the same space in the media as our 'freedom fighters'; both groups must operate as partners in development. The current media bias must end if the nation is to groom new leaders to take the baton from our political forefathers.

CHAPTER SIX

Cameraman turns Joy FM & Prime TV proprietor

“ I WISH those old MMD days could come back where the media was allowed to work freely and at the end of the year, we would receive letters and cards from the President to just say, 'Merry Christmas and Happy New Year," recalls Gerald Shawa, the proprietor Joy FM and Prime Television.

"Today, those things can't happen. Of course, we had challenges even then but not like this trouble we are in. The media is not safe."

Anti-apartheid icon Nelson Mandela once stated: "A critical, independent and investigative press is the lifeblood of any democracy". Indeed, a free, truthful, objective and growing press is the lifeblood of any democracy like Zambia's.

In 2008, while still employed as a cameraman for the Zambia National Broadcasting Corporation (ZNBC), Shawa felt the need to further grow a critical private media in Zambia. So, he started the process of securing a broadcasting licence with the Independent Broadcasting Authority

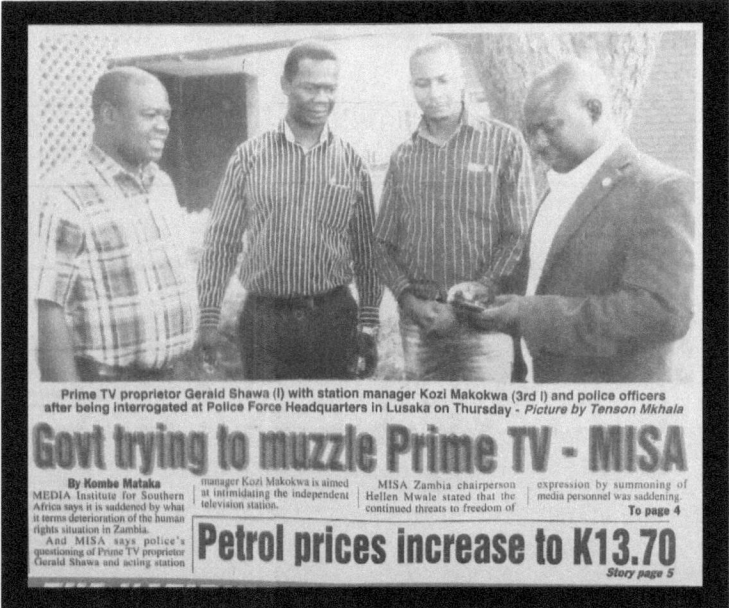

(IBA) that same year.

Shawa had great interest in setting up a television station owing to his enormous camera handling skills. However, his plans to establish a television station could not proceed because of the high costs involved in buying equipment and other logistics.

Having worked for the late Errol Hickey, the proprietor of Hickey Studios and Radio Phoenix, Shawa was energised to unfold his media entrepreneurial mind with a radio station he named Joy FM.

He continued pushing for a broadcasting licence as he awaited the arrival of radio equipment. When his equipment finally arrived, Shawa embarked on test transmissions until he was given a broadcasting licence in 2009. Joy FM was soon on the airwaves and later managed to secure its space in the competitive media business industry.

The determined media entrepreneur was convinced that there was still room in the industry for a new radio station.

"I was not intimidated by the number of radio stations that were already doing extremely well at that time because the cake is still very big. It's the way you package your services," he says. "Even if there are a lot of radio stations in the country today, the secret to making it in this industry is knowing what's common and that which is not there. I learnt a lot from Hickey Studios and Radio Phoenix."

Shawa ensured that Joy FM prioritised local content and promoted Zambian culture in its programming. Over his years of media practice, Shawa had observed that deejays on many radio stations were using fake accents and did not promote Zambian talent or culture. He, thus, set about reversing this trend.

"I make sure that my deejays speak as Zambians and do not use foreign accents on radio. I tell them, 'look, I hired you because I wanted you to promote the Zambian culture. And if I wanted to promote American and Nigerian culture, I would have hired Americans and Nigerians to do so. So just be normal,'" he says.

"The point is we must be identified by our own language and culture. Look at Nigerians and other African countries: their dress code and language identify who they are and what country they are coming from. That's what we need to do as a country with 72 tribes and a rich culture."

"The problem I have seen in this country is that when you speak your own language, you are seen to be dull and uneducated but that is wrong. We have to be proud of our own culture and speak our own languages. And that is the trend I and my station thought we could help alleviate, so we formed Joy FM."

In 2012, Shawa rekindled his plan to open a television station. The urge to start Prime Television had matured and he had already bought equipment to set it up.

The Ministry of Information and Broadcasting Services awarded the new television station a full broadcasting licence in 2013. Prime Television was launched and took its place in the nation's media industry. The television station placed priority on the promotion of Zambian culture and traditional music.

However, like many other media houses in Zambia, Prime Television has also been the subject of harassment and threatened closure by the government through the IBA.

"When it comes to a free press in Zambia, it is not very safe," said Shawa during an exclusive interview with me at his TV station on March 21, 2017.

"People are not able to report what is on the ground because there is no political leadership from the government. When these politicians are in the opposition, they make all sorts of promises that they don't come to do when they are in power. Free press bills have not been enacted up to now.

"In terms of the media, as journalists and media owners, we are not safe. First and foremost, we don't make enough money because of government interference and so, we can't pay our workers the desired salaries. We can't pay them what we don't make. We are not only there to disseminate information but to also make money to sustain us."

Below, Gerald Shawa shares with you the reader the challenges the private media has grappled with in recent times.

"You have seen in the recent past how journalists and media owners are summoned to the police. I was summoned to the police over a non-issue. But I was determined and knew that there was no case at all. The government didn't just want my station to cover the opposition. You have seen how we are beaten. We are not safe. Lesa Kasoma, director of Komboni Radio was beaten by police officers. We look forward to a day when the government in power can allow journalists and media houses to report things as they are without being intimidated or closed. The government must strive to promote freedom of expression, unlike the way things are now. Police officers beat journalists anyhow and the government does nothing about it. What we are praying for is a day when the existing leadership can promote freedom of the press; that is all we pray for."

"What the government wants is to have all media houses singing praise songs for them. They don't want any private media to accord a platform to people who may have divergent views from theirs. The moment you host persons other than them on a radio or television programme, they start calling in to question why you have done so."

According to Shawa, for a media house to realise any money, it unfortunately needs to be a platform for political rhetoric. If it features civic leaders or other politicians with divergent views, it risks being treated as an 'opposition propaganda tool'. He explained that to have any business as a media house, you need to have news bulletins that praise politicians in power every day.

Shawa told me he felt that when politicians are in government, they should be "servants of the people, work for the people and not their selfish aims." He added that when some of them are dismissed from government, they seek coverage from the very private media which they may previously have been trying so hard to get rid of, a trend he described as irrational.

Dismayed by the levels of intolerance of freedom of expression among leaders in the country, Shawa called for a ceasefire to what he termed "extreme media interference by government." He said it was not the government's role to decide for advertisers which media houses to work with. He has observed that the government has in the recent past intimidated both public and private entities that place adverts in private media houses as a way of fixing the critical press.

"...private entities that advertise with us, because of knowing how sensitive the government is with criticism, the moment they know there is a story with divergent views and we have their advert, they call to demand us to drop the story or they pull down the advert. So it's a matter of making tough choices for our survival in the private sector. Government interferes with all private businesses that advertise with us to issue threats of closure if they don't stop advertising with us, simply because 'we make life difficult for them'," Shawa said.

The audience will determine the future of news

Today's social media readership comments are mostly on issues to do with sex, witchcraft, rumours, 'miracles' among non-issues that take rounds on the fora.

Daily, people capture and share videos and pictures and upload them onto Facebook, Twitter and Instagram among other social media platforms. This has contributed to the booming of citizen journalism. The public today devotes attention to what they want to read, watch and listen to. The agenda-setting role that the traditional media seemed to have enjoyed in years gone by is diminishing each day. The emergence of social media in Zambia has posed both advantages and disadvantages towards the industry and society at large.

New technology has to some extent replaced the old system that financed traditional media operations. Back in the days, mainstream media benefited from all that had to do with advertising to a huge audience. This is because social media platforms like Facebook have assumed the roles that the mainstream platforms possessed. This has led to lowered revenues for the mainstream media, thereby affecting the number of workers that it can employ. This has the potential of reducing the number of journalists needed to occupy a newsroom, meaning that people would at some point have to stop aspiring to be journalists, a situation that would not benefit this country.

So, Zambia's newsrooms are getting significantly smaller every year because of the straightforwardness of the news gathering environment.

For example, today if police officers kill a person during a protest or riot, they would not lie and say the protestor died after he or she jumped off a building. This is because citizen journalism does its best in documenting events that may occur before the traditional media arrives on the scene. So, this eases the work of a journalist who most often get to social media to get information that they, in turn, begin to follow-up on.

The levels of citizen journalism in Zambia, as with other parts of the world, have also given rise to irresponsible reporting. Gone are the days when the traditional media decided what the public could or could not see, read or not read. We had a set of responsible gatekeepers but today because of social media, anyone can decide to post whatever pictures or articles they may have access to, regardless of the nature or sensitivity of the content. For example, pictures of the dead in caskets or hospitals, pictures of sexually abused minors at court and explicit videos among many social media abuses.

Thus, the days of telling the public what to think about are over. The public is thinking about what it feels it should think about, hence political or economic activism programmes do not grasp their attention.

You will agree that the future of news is gravely being determined by the audience. And because of this, news in the future has to be presented in a much more different style. Social media is dominantly carrying most breaking news stories that in the past were carried by newspapers. This also makes it difficult for a media outlet like the print media to carry in its editions the same stories that may have made the rounds on social media the previous day.

However, the boom in social media also has many benefits. It is now difficult for propaganda or indoctrination to succeed. People have various platforms on which to cross-check the information given to them by a particular media house. Today, even if social media trending issues are largely bent on trivial matters, it has quite effectively united Zambia. We are able to know what is happening in remote areas like Shang'ombo in seconds because of the important role that social media is playing.

Therefore, instead of concentrating their energies on rumour-mongering or gossip, the youth should use social media platforms to earn a living by advertising their entrepreneurial endeavours. They can also use such platforms to hold leaders accountable and make them honour their campaign promises by constantly exposing under-development or injustices in their communities. It is up to you and me to take up the mantle and bring about the change that we want to see.

CHAPTER SEVEN

The election of an accomplished liar

WHOEVER gets elected as councillor, council chairperson, mayor, parliamentarian, or as president today, is either an accomplished charmer or liar.

Ronald Bailey, an award-winning science correspondent for Reason magazine, quotes political thinkers in the write-up Why All Politicians Lie published on *reason.com* in 2012 as having said that, Lying, along with capacity for back-biting, obfuscating and double-dealing, seems to be a qualification for politicians.

Have you tried to find out why politicians lie? And why do you think leaders need to have a high level of integrity-honesty? Well, you don't need to hit your head against the wall nor scratch it while gazing at the ceiling. The reason is simple; we live in a world where every one of them wants to rule as correctly observed by slain South African Reggae artiste Lucky Dube in one of his songs on the 'Respect' album. This is despite some of them having a severe deficiency of leadership skills.

Integrity is among the top leadership qualities that one aspiring to preside over the affairs of others needs to possess or learn.

You may and may not agree with the above notion. But the questions on whether we have leaders or managers for President in Zambia pop up to help us to try and understand our current scenario as a country.

If we do have leaders, do we have people with a mind to critically analyse which leaders deserve a mandate before we vote for them? And if we do, what kind of 'leadership' qualities do Zambian voters go for? And do we even understand who a leader is?

But before we proceed to understanding the discourse, I have two more questions for you: Have you ever wondered what it is like to be a leader? Do you want to be a leader? And I know in your heart, you may be saying, 'I don't want to be a leader, it's not my thing'. But a leader isn't always just someone who is in a position of President, university principal, lawyer, teacher and mayor or school prefect. A leader is anyone possessing among the main qualities, humility and integrity. With that said, today you can be a leader for someone or group of people.

It is important to mention that not all people in authority are leaders. Really, you don't need to have a title to be a leader. You too can be a leader provided you're honest with yourself and others; reliable, respectful, patient and hard working.

This argument can be backed by citing a well-thought-out argument by Francis Chishala, a Catholic priest who states in his book A Robust Think Tank for Africa that *"Leadership is not about having a position or role of authority, but it is about a person's ability to influence others whatever the situation or place in the organisation or society. Not all people with positions of authority are leaders; many are simply managers."*

Leadership styles vary. But with specific concerns for Zambia, a 'Christian Nation', with a fledgling democracy, leadership must be that which influences people to willingly move with you, free of intimidation and filled with a passion to work with you.

You see, when one is voted into public office as a leader, it does not entail that you preside over people's affairs in any manner you wish! If you do that, you are literally supposed to be arrested for abusing the powers they lend you during an election.

Being president, parliamentarian, mayor, council chairperson and councillor is very different from being a manager at your own firm, bar or farm. There is a distinction that politicians need to see. When you are elected by the people, you can do all things you desire, provided you have been permitted to do so by the people through constant consultation. And one way to do this is through referendums.

It is argued that Zambia has struggled to produce a leader the people can always trust and believe in. During campaigns, candidates attempt to woo votes from unsuspecting people. They buy alcohol for the youth and the elderly, distribute mealie-meal and cash and ultimately emerge winners of an election.

But when they finally get to Lusaka—the seat of State House and Parliament—they stop trying to woo votes and the people's woes begin. However true this is, we cannot blame these power-hungry people alone in this situation but collectively blame the voters and the 'liars'. This is so because the 'leaders' we have today are not aliens. They are raised and nurtured in our homes. And the leadership 'crisis' we may have in Zambia is coming from our individual houses.

As parents, how have we nurtured our children? Do we correct our children when they do wrong? Do we punish them when they steal from another or perhaps we instead shield them when they do so? Do we preach to them on the importance of extended families? Do we help them realise on the importance of helping those who may not have, even within our homes?

If we do, then what is the problem? And if we don't, do we expect our children to be smart-minded people when they assume positions requiring leadership, knowing we failed to equip them with the building blocks necessary to become morally upright leaders? This is the genesis of the many problems Zambia is facing. Our morals are eroding at a very high rate and therefore, chances of having a genuine future leader are equally growing thinner each day.

Our communities these days do not pay attention to nurturing another parent's child as it used to before. In the past, a child from one house in a community was regarded as everyone's responsibility with regards to ensuring conformity to morals in society. Today, that is not the case, hence the growing breakdown in the extended family system. And this has contributed to the rapid erosion of morals.

This calls for concerted efforts from every one of us in these communities because this problem can and will not be dealt with adequately if we leave it to others. Today you may say 'it is not my problem because it does not affect me directly', but remember that this problem has a potential to creep into your household tomorrow or in the farther future.

The lying politician, therefore, is birthed from our homes. Greedy and rigid people are birthed from our houses and our community. The 'liars' that tour villages when it's election time, the people that come to your doorstep dressed in cheap chequered jackets and buy you and me intoxicating liquor, give us a few 'kwachas' and show us their funny dances, are a product of our communities.

Those that receive these 'bribes'—the alcohol, mealie-meal, cash, etc—are people whose morals may have been eroded due to high levels of poverty.

If our country is to make progress, we all have to start raising our children in a manner that will save and serve society. Society will be saved if we as a people begin to impart good morals in our children, nurturing them in a manner acceptable to God and the community.

One would eventually want to level blame on ancestors that birthed and nurtured this generation of lying 'leaders', but that would not be a logical thing to do because of some 'untruth-fools' we have today. The environment they were brought up in may have contributed to making them who they are.

Politicians are not aliens; they and all dictators come from our homes and communities.

Zambia still has a chance to have a 'cream' of leaders to oversee its affairs in the democratic and Christian and humane manner that it deserves. As a nation we need to remain committed to principles of democracy, humanity and Christianity. And the way we treat each other, be it our perceived enemies or best of friends, leaves much to be desired.

We must rebuild our Zambia, we must re-establish our democracy.

Zambia shall be rebuilt if we begin to question those that aspire to lead us. We must see real leadership qualities and not just being bought a bag of mealie-meal. Let's get back to our homes and talk politics!

You may not be affected by today's problems because you may probably be on their side but believe this; one day, it may not be you to face the problems or your children, but a generation that your children will birth. Look at how the three quarters of the people in this country are struggling to access affordable health services! Look at how our mothers in our villages are struggling to have a meal per day!

Year in, year out, some untruthful politicians visit our mothers, give them false hope, lie to them and tell them they will change things once voted into office but once they have the mandate, some of them never go back to the people. They instead sit in Parliament enacting laws that call for allowance increments, among other petty issues, while the people who vote for them struggle to educate their children because there are no schools in their areas.

Zambia must be rebuilt. We are the generation to stop a crop of politicians that mean to do nothing, but lying to our citizenry. We must protect our future generations; they must never inherit the problems we are wallowing in today. We must focus our attention on better candidates that will take the spirit to better Zambia. This country can wear a smile again if we continue to vote for leaders with a vision for posterity, a leadership with a heart for the youth.

And like Ronald Bailey rightly observed in '*Why All Politicians lie*', indeed honesty is not inherent in electoral politics. Perhaps someday disgusted voters will revolt and rein in the size and scope of government. Until that happy day, the only recourse of an appalled citizenry is to throw in the towel a crop of double-dealing leaders who become too outrageous.

The people will only come to know lies when journalists that report politics get acquainted with a wide array of information in a country like Zambia. When a scribe has information on their finger-tips as they interview politicians or civic leaders, they have to be brave, challenge and collect correct information beneficial to the potential voter.

Unemployment, '*Wako ni Wako*' in governments

Like youthful leadership, this country is in dire need of entrepreneurial minds. We need people to think beyond being employed by the government. We need students to venture into fields of study that when completed will further create employment for the thousands wandering the streets of this country. There is just so much over-dependence on the government for employment, but the government can only take so much because of *wako ni wako*.

It is for this reason that the youth of today must begin to think about areas to exploit instead of government jobs. This is the mind that the 21st century calls for. However, we cannot run away from the fact that governments have had misplaced priorities that have in turn led to the depletion of the treasury. The government cannot employ as much as it used to in the past because of directing funds towards unnecessary expenditures as some people have argued.

The government has a duty and mandate to employ people in the civil service. The government of Zambia under the PF has to some extent provided employment and has largely struggled to employ the numbers of youths as it envisioned in the run-up to the 2011 general polls.

Today, some government officials are heard encouraging the youth in the country to set up businesses, have entrepreneurial minds and quit over-dependence on government recruitments. This is very good; the youth must refocus their lines of thought on jobs. However, while some government officials encourage the youth to be entrepreneurs

CHAPTER SEVEN

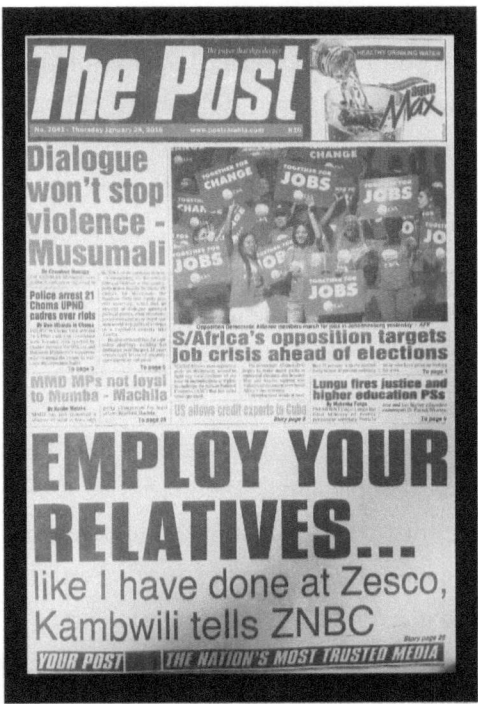

when they are on the podium, behind the scenes they employ their own children in the civil service.

They encourage *bana baba nzao* (other people's children) to start businesses without empowerment and on the other side, they hand-pick their relatives and give them government jobs, making *wako ni wako* (your own tribesmen) prominent in the civil service. This has led to low productivity levels in the civil service. Some of the government officials or ministers' relatives have no skills at all. They are dull and cannot manage the civil service efficiently! Government has lost colossal sums of money because of some selfish officials employing incompetent people in fields that require competition.

Nepotism and vindictiveness is what one can associate successive governments to. If you are not connected to any 'big fish', oftenly, you shall wallow in unemployment until God Almighty comes to your aid. And because of the hype tribalism has been given in this country, if you belong to a certain 'condemned region', you will not be employed or if you were in employment and do not dance to the tune of the government of the day, you are bound to be retired in 'national interest'. Zambia must be rebuilt to restore sanity and the spirit of unity.

President Edgar Lungu, in his state of the nation address in Parliament on March 17, 2017, advised the civil service to employ people on merit and to never discriminate anyone on the basis of tribe. This in itself confirms that there has been massive nepotism and tribalism in the government and the President wants the vice to end.

Former Post managing editor and now local government permanent secretary, Amos Malupenga in his book, 'L*evy Patrick Mwanawasa: An Incentive for Posterity*', quotes President Mwanawasa confirming massive tribalism and nepotism in the Frederick Chiluba government and said in his defence, "*What has happened is that in my government, I have destroyed the empire because (then) to be appointed in the foreign service during the last regime, you had to be Bemba. If the Ambassador was not Bemba, the deputy had to be Bemba.*"

Mwanawasa admitted that tribalism existed in the Chiluba government. And at some point he too was accused of being tribal, an allegation he denied. Tribalism has been a long standing issue in Zambian politics. But this tribalism talk in African politics has the potential to divide countries and further ignite confusion. This is why there is need to criminalise tribal talk, like racial talk is outlawed in some countries.

If we don't, before the country realises it, we would have lost the unity and peace we have enjoyed this far. We are One Zambia, One Nation. Therefore, people must vote and be employed based on one's capabilities in a specified area. And the media can help end tribal talk by politicians that thrive on it, unlike the current situation that seems to be igniting the talk to please those they want to remain in power or get into power. However, if the media also concentrates on reporting on who has said what about what tribe, such talk could ruin this country.

CHAPTER SEVEN

The end of a lying politician

The ultimate end of a lying politician will never please his supporters. The long court processes become the order of the liar's life and all the stolen money gets directed towards legal fees and paying *ng'wang'wazis* to show support when they appear for trials at courts. But at some point, the numbers of supporters shrink as the money diminishes.

The fraudsters' lies catch up with them. What a sad ending this shall be for lovers of violence, corruption, murder and lying!

Have you ever wondered why revolutionists like Fidel Castro and Che Guevara were never referred to as politicians? Well, they meant what they said when they pushed for revolutions. A politician is associated with promising the unattainable to unsuspecting people. Politicians are associated with rhetoric they do not even understand.

When a politician visits you, question their visit. When they constantly ring and want to associate with you, be concerned. They use people to get to the top and when they get there, they become 'busy'. Journalists, as we have already alluded to, enjoy relationships with 'powerful' people in society—the politicians.

Politicians are a 'clever' set of individuals; they are determined to get what they want when they want it but not every one of them gets it. These are the kinds of people that will befriend a journalist, give them a few 'kwachas', and in turn, the reporter does public relations stories for them. It's practically impossible for a reporter to write exposés or comments against his/her paymaster. One's conscience, that's if they even have one, cannot permit it.

Meanwhile, when a politician gets what they may have wanted, they abandon the reporters and stop picking up their calls. Reporters feel betrayed but a politician cannot be blamed much for this act of selfishness. Journalists are the eyes of the people in society. People have so much faith in our journalists, some of whom of late have been a disappointment. We as journalists have not done enough for the majority of Zambians living in abject poverty, people living with disabilities, children and women. We have not adequately highlighted the many challenges the other side of society has been facing.

We have concentrated so much on the public figures, who most of the times want to be praised in stories. We as a Zambian media must restore our moral conscience and for once report on issues that affect our communities. We can't afford to continue to betray our brothers and sisters in our communities for whom we exist to serve.

We must wake up or our fate will be like that of a lying politician that goes to the vulnerable to ask for votes. When politicians tour villages to ask for votes, they are the ones that kneel before you. When they have been elected, it becomes your turn to kneel before them and ask them to sink a borehole they may have promised during their campaign. Alas, they do not fulfil many of their promises. You cannot even reach them via phone to remind them of their promises. They are too 'busy' with meetings discussing how to 'bring' development to your area.

These politicians abandon the voters. The only time they get back to their constituencies, towns and villages is during another season of elections. Most Zambian politicians are crafty human beings. Very few of them have a genuine heart for the people they claim they want to serve. They are like some media houses and agenda setting, who prioritise things they want; that is their business interests. But the ordinary Zambian that spends hours on queues to vote for them is the one that suffers. An old woman that wakes up early on election morning, abandoning her small-scale farming activities just to be on that queue to put you—the politician in office, suffers the most.

But do these politicians have morals? Do these people have a conscience? When a person pursues a political career, do they cease being human? Because the hearts and colours they show after elections are somewhat inhuman.

As a people, we can bring an end to this. There is no way that in almost all the elections, all the ordinary person can point to is party regalia and more hunger. More hunger because during elections, these politicians buy food and alcohol and dance with the people all the time, leaving little time for the poor villager or youth to work. And when the people they danced with leave for Lusaka, the people remain in poverty.

This kind of a politician's ending will not please ears that will hear of it. Sooner than later, the Zambian people will rise and say no to more lies. The Zambian people, whom politicians have taken advantage of for some time, have a watchful eye.

The media must learn many lessons and expose abuse of office, violation of human rights and corruption without fear of being victimised. Once exposed, these vices will take the lying politician to the courts of law. The courts of law shall have sober legal-minded people. The political landscape in this country is ever changing. People are not as ignorant as they may have been five years ago. People are simply tired of lies, they want real change spearheaded by out leaders. They do not want party chitenge materials. They want schools, hospitals, safe drinking water, better sanitation, jobs and the opportunity to start up their own businesses.

The Zambian people want policies that will benefit everyone in their communities. Long gone are the days when lies got a 'leader' into office. Be wary of a democratic revolution that will one day take accomplished liars to jail. This shall be the end of a lying politician.

Now is the beginning of the ending of the era where electoral votes were wooed by lies and giving false hope to the vulnerable. And the ultimate destination of a lying politician is nothing better than jail. Lying is a sin whose wages is death. Lengthy court processes can be a cause of one's death or bankruptcy. This generation of the young shall not bend the laws. It shall uphold the provisions of the Constitution and improve upon the bill of rights.

The emerging youthful leadership shall ensure that corrupt minds and accomplished fraudsters are jailed when found guilty. Ultimately, like they say, the leaders we have in power today, whether good or bad, are a reflection of the society they are found in. We get the leaders we deserve!

AUTOBIOGRAPHY

I T WAS on January 7, 1989 when Agnes Bwembya Bwalya, a Bemba of Kasama in Northern Province, gave birth to me in Mansa, Luapula Province. I was one of seven children born to her and Hagai Kashiki Senior, a Zambia National Service (ZNS) officer from Kisanswe-Kasempa in North-Western Province.

They got married in 1974 and being a man in uniform, he was often posted to different parts of the country on duty. My earliest memories were of my family frequently being transferred around the country and I grew to appreciate early on in my young life the importance of the many tribes Zambia is blessed with.

I started grade one at Lima Primary School in Kitwe District in 1996. When I reached grade three, my father retired from ZNS and used part of his pension to buy a house in Kitwe's Ndeke Changa-Changa Township. I continued with my education at Ndeke Basic School where, because I hadn't understood much during grade 5, I decide to repeat grade 4, without my parents' knowledge.

I eventually told them of what I had done and to my surprise, they just laughed about it, assuaging my fears. Because of what I had done, I did not sit for the grade seven exams in 2002 as I should have; instead, I did so in 2003. I passed my exams and went to grade eight at Wesley Nyirenda Basic School in 2004 , from there I was eventually selected to go to grade 10 at Kitwe Boys Secondary School in 2006.

However, due to my being in Lusaka over the holidays, I started school at St Charles' Catholic School. The school had challenges having teachers on a regular basis due to lack of funding. So, I told my older sister, Patricia about the situation that I was faced with and immediately, we started looking for a different school. At this point, I had developed an interest in going to a boarding school.

Through the help of my brother-in-law, Michael Daka, I managed to secure a place at Mansa Secondary School in Luapula Province—my place of birth—in 2007. Instead of being enrolled in grade 11, I was asked to repeat grade 10 because the head teacher thought I hadn't learned much at my previous school. Without hesitation, I agreed and repeated grade 10.

While at Mansa Secondary School, I was appointed as prefect and given extra responsibilities of being house captain of my dormitory. This was in late 2008 to 2009, the year when I sat for my grade 12 examinations. As I waited for the results to be released, I participated as an enumerator in the 2010 National Census for the Central Statistical Office in Chililabombwe District. And after the grade 12 results were released that same year, my thoughts to study journalism blossomed. So, I registered to study journalism at the Zambia Institute of Mass Communication (ZAMCOM).

REFERENCES

Amos Malupenga, (2009), *Levy Patrick Mwanawasa: Incentive for Posterity*, NISC (pty) Grahamstown

Francis Chishala, (2014), *A Robust Think Tank for Africa: Words of Hope, Ingenuity and Faith*, Partridge Africa Publishing.

Mike Hall, (*The Post* 2004), *How The Post Was Born*, The Post Zambia Limited Lumumba Road, Lusaka.

Kevin D. Williamson, (2011), *The Politically Incorrect Guide to Socialism*. Regnery Publishing, Inc.

Richard Sakala, (2009), *A Mockery Of Justice – Rule Without Law Legacy 2001-2008*, Sentor Publishers, Lusaka.

The Post (issue number 2699), March 8, 2004

http://www.nytimes.com/1991/11/13/world/newspaper-gains-zambia-s-respect.html

https://www.spj.org/ethics-papers—politics.asp

https://www.google.co.zm/amp/reason.com/archives/2012/11/06/why-all-politicians-lie/amp

Thomas Nelson, (1994), *The Holy Bible, New King James Version*

http://www.opensecrects.org/news/2010/09/media-professionals-and-journalists-donate/

http://zambiareports.com/2016/06/27/president-lungu-respond-to-diplomats-pay-the-post-debt-it-will-re-opne/

www.ingramcontent.com/pod-product-compliance
Lightning Source LLC
Chambersburg PA
CBHW031417210526
45464CB00005B/1926